ABOUT BRITAIN NO. 3

HOME COUNTIES

WITH A PORTRAIT BY R.S.R.FITTER

PUBLISHED FOR

THE FESTIVAL OF BRITAIN OFFICE   *FENTON*

COLLINS 14 ST JAMES'S PL

THE ABOUT BRITAIN GUIDES

List of Titles

1. WEST COUNTRY. *Portrait by* Geoffrey Grigson. *Cornwall: Devonshire: Somerset: Gloucestershire: N.W. Wiltshire.*

2. WESSEX. *Portrait by* Geoffrey Grigson. *S.E. Wiltshire: Dorset: Hampshire: Isle of Wight.*

3. HOME COUNTIES. *Portrait by* R. S. R. Fitter. *Sussex: Surrey: Kent: London: Middlesex: East Berkshire: S.E. Buckinghamshire: Hertfordshire: S.W. Essex.*

4. EAST ANGLIA. *Portrait by* R. H. Mottram. *N.E. Essex: Suffolk: Norfolk: Cambridgeshire: Huntingdonshire: Soke of Peterborough: Holland (Lincs.)*

5. CHILTERNS TO BLACK COUNTRY. *Portrait by* W. G. Hoskins. *West Berkshire: Oxfordshire: North Buckinghamshire: Bedfordshire: Northamptonshire (excluding Corby area): Warwickshire: Worcestershire: Staffordshire.*

6. SOUTH WALES AND THE MARCHES. *Portrait by* W. J. Gruffydd. *Pembrokeshire: Caermarthenshire: Glamorgan: Monmouthshire: Brecknockshire: Cardiganshire: Radnorshire: Herefordshire.*

7. NORTH WALES AND THE MARCHES. *Portrait by* W. J. Gruffydd. *Montgomeryshire: Merionethshire: Caernarvonshire: Anglesey: Denbighshire: Flintshire: Shropshire: Cheshire.*

8. EAST MIDLANDS AND THE PEAK. *Portrait by* W. G. Hoskins. *Leicestershire: Lincolnshire (except Holland): Rutland: Corby area of Northamptonshire: Nottinghamshire: Derbyshire.*

9. LANCASHIRE AND YORKSHIRE. *Portrait by* Leo Walmsley. *Most of Yorkshire: Lancashire except Lake District.*

10. LAKES TO TYNESIDE. *Portrait by* Sid Chaplin. *Cumberland: Westmorland: Lake District (Lancashire): Part of North Riding (Yorkshire): Durham: Northumberland: Isle of Man.*

11. LOWLANDS OF SCOTLAND. *Portrait by* John R. Allan.

12. HIGHLANDS AND ISLANDS OF SCOTLAND. *Portrait by* Alastair M. Dunnett.

13. NORTHERN IRELAND. *Portrait by* E. Estyn Evans.

The Relief Maps used for the covers and jackets of these books were designed and produced by Geographical Projects Ltd.

Produced by A. N. Holden & Co. Ltd., London, and printed in England by Sun Printers Ltd., London and Watford. Published by Wm. Collins Sons & Co., Ltd., in 1951.

The North Downs near Otford.

LIST OF PHOTOGRAPHERS

A SHORT READING LIST

Arnold, Ralph. *The Hundred of Hoo.* Constable. 1947. 12s. 6d.

Betjeman, J., and Piper, J. *Murray's Berkshire Architectural Guide.* 1949. 18s.

Betjeman, J., and Piper, J. *Murray's Buckinghamshire Architectural Guide.* 1948. 15s.

Brett-James, N. G. *The Growth of Stuart London.* Allen & Unwin. 1935. 25s.

Cunningham, G. H. *London: A Survey of Buildings and Monuments.* Dent. 1931. 10s. 6d.

Curwen, E. C. *The Archaeology of Sussex.* Methuen. 1937. 12s. 6d.

Fitter, R. S. R. *London's Birds.* Collins. 1949. 10s. 6d.

Fitter, R. S. R. *London's Natural History.* New Naturalist Series. Collins. 1945. 21s.

Forshaw, J. H., and Abercrombie, L. P. *The County of London Plan.* Macmillan. 1943. 12s. 6d.

Gibbings, R. *Sweet Thames Run Softly.* Dent. 1940. 12s. 6d.

Gillham, E. H., and Holmes, R. C. *The Birds of the North Kent Marshes.* Collins. 1950. 12s. 6d.

Herbert, J. *Port of London.* Britain in Pictures Series. Collins. 1948. 5s.

Jessup, R. F. *The Archaeology of Kent.* Methuen. 1930. 10s. 6d.

Margary, I. D. *Roman Ways in the Weald.* Phoenix House. 1948. 25s.

Mortimer, J. D. *An Anthology of the Home Counties.* Methuen. 1947. 10s. 6d.

Muirhead, F., and Russell, R. *London and its Environs.* (With Atlas and 33 maps and plans.) Blue Guide Series. Ernest Benn. 1935. 21s.

Piper, John. *Romney Marsh.* King Penguin. 1950. 3s.

Rasmussen, S. E. *London: the unique city.* Cape (2nd Edition). 1948. 18s.

Stamp, Dudley, L. *The Land of Britain Series.* Geographical Publications Ltd.

Straker, E. *Wealden Iron.* A history of the former ironworks in Sussex, Surrey and Kent, from the earliest times to their cessation. Bell. 1931. 15s.

Summerson, J. *Georgian London.* Pleiades. 1946. 21s.

Vulliamy, C. E. *Archaeology of Middlesex and London.* Methuen. 1930. 10s. 6d.

The *County Books* series. (Sussex, Surrey, Kent, South London, East London, Middlesex, Buckinghamshire, Hertfordshire, Essex and The Western Reaches.) Illustrated and with folding map. Robert Hale. 15s. each.

The *Companion Into* series. (Sussex, Surrey, Kent, Essex, Buckinghamshire.) Illustrated, and with an end-paper map. Methuen. 10s. 6d. each.

The *Highways and Byways* series. (Surrey and Sussex.) Originally printed in 1900 and, reprinted in 1950. Macmillan. 10s. 6d.

MAPS

Excellent maps for the whole of Britain are published by the Ordnance Survey and by Bartholomew. The most useful for travellers are the one-inch and the quarter-inch series. In addition, a series of special maps is published by the Ordnance Survey, each covering Britain in two sheets on the scale of 1/625,000 (about ten miles to one inch). This series includes: 'Coal and Iron', 'Land Classification', 'Land Utilization', 'Railways', 'Types of Farming', 5s. per sheet; and 'Solid Geology', 12s. 6d. per sheet.

An orchard in the rich lands of Kent.

USING THIS BOOK

THIS GUIDE-BOOK is one of a series 'About Britain,' so we hope, in a new way. Like the others (there are thirteen altogether) it contains many photographs, a map, a gazetteer, and illustrated strip-maps of the most convenient itineraries. And it begins with a portrait of the district—an account of many of the facts about it which are worth knowing and many of the things which are worth seeing.

This does not explain the newness. These guides have been prompted by the Festival of Britain. The Festival shows how the British people, with their energy and natural resources, contribute to civilization. So the guide-books as well celebrate a European country alert, ready for the future, and strengthened by a tradition which you can *see* in its remarkable monuments and products of history and even pre-history. If the country includes Birmingham, Glasgow or Belfast, it includes Stonehenge. If it contains Durham Cathedral, it contains coal mines, iron foundries, and the newest of factories devising all the goods of a developing civilization. If it includes remnants of medieval forest, it includes also the new forests of conifers transforming acres of useless land. It contains art galleries and wild scenery, universities and remote villages, great ports and small fishing harbours, shrines of national sentiment and institutes of scientific research—the past and the present. On the Downs in Wiltshire we can stand on a minute plot of ground on which the Iron Age farmer reaped his corn with a sickle, and watch a few yards away a combine harvester steadily devouring ripe acres of wheat.

What we are as a people, where we have our homes, what we do, what we make—cotton in Lancashire, tin plate in South Wales, cars outside Oxford, mustard or clothes in Norwich, woollens in Bradford —depends all of it upon a thousand national peculiarities, of soil, vegetation, minerals, water, ways of transport, the continuity and the accidents of history.

It is this living country of today which these guide-books emphasize, the place and the people, not only the country of the past or the exquisitely varied landscape of fields and moors and mountains and coast. They are handbooks for the explorer. The aim is to show what Britain is now, in the North, the Midlands and the South, in East Anglia and the West, in Wales, Scotland, Northern Ireland, and to explain something of the why and wherefore. To investigate this Britain the sensible explorer has to take to the roads and the by-roads. This accounts for the itineraries and the strip-maps, which have been devised to guide you, if you need them, as simply, quickly and comprehensively as possible through the districts portrayed by word and illustration in each book.

The Festival of Britain belongs to 1951. But we hope these explorers' handbooks will be useful far beyond the Festival year.

Thames Tug and barges loaded with Esparto Grass

HOME COUNTIES

A PORTRAIT OF LONDON AND THE SOUTH-EAST

BY R.S.R.FITTER

The South Downs overlooking a harvest field near Lewes.

KENT is the gateway to England, and London is the gateway to the world. Men first walked into Britain across the chalk downs that linked Calais to Dover until little more than 7,000 years ago. Even when a general lowering of the land surface led first to the flooding of the North Sea and then to the breach in the chalk ridge which has since widened into the modern Strait of Dover, men were still lured into England along the Kentish shore by the sight of its gleaming white cliffs, the cliffs that gave England its ancient name of Albion, so clear on a fine day from the coast of France. A constant stream of invaders, Stone Age men, Bronze Age men, Celts, Belgae, Romans, Jutes, Saxons, Normans, have landed on the open shores of Kent and Sussex. From them all emerged the mongrel race of the English, fertile in ideas and achievement as only a cross-bred race can be. Over the centuries they have used the focal position of the first practicable bridge-way over the Thames to build one of the half-dozen greatest cities the world has ever known.

To London came, and come, the traders of the world, bringing much of the wealth of the world. From London go forth a stream of merchandise and services, and the fertilizing power of intangible monetary capital. And all the time London remains, like an ancient jewel, encrusted with cobwebs and verdigris, yet set in one of the fairest countrysides that the accidents of nature and the art of man have ever managed to contrive. Even after a hundred years of the overspilling of the great Wen against which Cobbett already railed, and 30 years of almost uncontrolled peppering of the countryside with gimcrack and tasteless building, the fields and woods and heaths of the Home Counties

7

can still challenge comparison with any other part of the British Isles for rich and varied scenery, prosperous and efficient agriculture, and a fascinating variety of wild life.

There are really two regions in the south-east corner of England, divided by the North Downs. The valley of the lower Thames, known to geographers as the London Basin, is a huge, flat saucer of chalk, open at one end, on which some fifty to sixty million years ago immemorial seas deposited a succession of sands and clays. The rims of the saucer are formed by the crests and escarpments of the Chilterns to the north and the North Downs to the south, and it opens to the sea in the flat marshlands of Essex and northern Kent. The deposits of sand have yielded some of the most characteristic features of the region, notably the pine and heather-covered heaths of eastern Berkshire and north-west Surrey, now being progressively partitioned among the military, the foresters and the builders. Sands of various kinds also cap the hills that rise from the Thames plain on either side of central London, Hampstead and Highgate on the north and the Crystal Palace ridge on the south, bereft since 1936 of the great glass dome, relic of the Great Exhibition of 1851, which had stood there for 80 years. At a much later period than the laying down of the sands, almost yesterday to the geologists, perhaps a hundred thousand years ago, the Thames, which had been occupying a far wider bed than it does to-day, began to cut its way down to its present bed, leaving three terraces of gravel behind to mark its stages. These gravel terraces are of the utmost importance to our story, for on them began human settlement in the Lower Thames Valley. Every time you walk down the Strand you are treading one of these ancient terraces, laid down between the third and fourth phases of the Ice Age; and the steep descent down Villiers Street or Savoy Hill will remind you that only a couple of thousand years ago here was a little cliff or grassy bank down to the water's edge. Even as late as the middle of the last century the high tide still lapped at the buildings where now stands the Savoy Hotel, for the Victoria Embankment was not completed till 1870.

The other region of the south-east is an eroded dome, better known as the Weald, completely encompassed by the chalk scarps of the North and South Downs, except at its seaward end, and stretching "twixt Rake and Rye, Black Down and Beachy Head', though, of course, it covers much of Kent and Surrey as well as Kipling's favourite Sussex. In the Weald the chalk, which must originally have made an impressive mountain, has been worn down by some millions of years of weathering to reveal the clays and sands beneath. This soft, white rock, which has begotten fully half the beauty of south-east England, once lay flat and oozy on the floor of a sea that covered much of southern England seventy million or more years ago. Millions of years later still came one of those gigantic earth-movements which make all

8

Bluebells in a beech wood at Amersham.

The Seven Sisters, near Seaford.

our modern scientific wonders shrink to Lilliputian proportions. In Asia it upreared the Himalayas; in Middle Europe it created the Alps; on the extreme western border of the Eurasian land-mass it crinkled the chalk, hundreds of feet thick, as a man would press a concertina. In the Isle of Wight the earth-storm gave us the superb chalk cliffs terminating in the Needles, where the crinkle is almost vertical. Further east the concertina was less compressed, and the flat layer of chalk was merely bent into a gentle horizontal S. On the clays and sands which later accumulated in the northern and concave half of the S, Greater London now stands. The convex southern loop of the S was worn right away, nature being a great leveller, so that now the vast whale-back of chalk soaring into the sky from Firle Beacon northward to Chevening Park exists only in the mind's eye of some geologist-poet on an April day.

Between the scarp slopes of the two ranges of downs, some of them steep to the point of precipitousness, lie the sands and clays of the Weald, laid down millions of years before the chalk, in concentric horseshoes. Some are quite narrow bands, as the upper greensand and gault clay usually are at the foot of the downs, but others swell out into extensive tracts. Such is the lower greensand, which creates the rolling heaths around Hindhead and Thursley, including the famous Devil's Punchbowl, and passes on eastwards to achieve the greatest altitude in our area, 965 feet at Leith Hill, which is crowned by

The Long Man of Wilmington, a figure cut in the chalk (see page 27).

a tower said to bring the observer up to the 1,000-foot mark. From here there is a superb view over the whole of the western Weald, and on a clear day you may glimpse the Channel through the Adur gap at Shoreham, 25 miles away. Within the lower greensand comes a more low-lying vale of clay, once a great tropical lake bordered by jungles full of giant dinosaurs, iguanodons and the like, later the dense oak forest of Andreadswald, pierced until the Middle Ages only by Stane Street and a few other Roman roads; it is still the most thickly wooded part of the British Isles. The core of the whole Wealden area is the high sandstone ridge, rising to nearly 800 feet at Crowborough, which gives open moorland on Ashdown Forest, but is well wooded farther west, in the Forests of Worth, Tilgate and St Leonards.

PILTDOWN MAN AND SWANSCOMBE MAN

Though of great importance for the prehistorian, England of the Home Counties contains comparatively few prehistoric sites or sights that are worth a quick visit. Gazing at the holes in the ground whence came such venerable old gentlemen as Swanscombe Man and Piltdown Man is rather to be compared with examining the beds in which Queen Elizabeth is said to have slept than with the real cultural comprehension which comes from seeing for oneself such titanic monuments of antiquity as Stonehenge or Avebury. The site at Piltdown, not far from Uckfield in East Sussex, where the famous skull was found in 1912, has rightly been proposed for preservation as a 'geological monument', in order that future discoveries there may be safeguarded, though the most modern methods of research, which depend on the fact that the fluorine content of bones increases with geological age, have now shown that Piltdown Man most likely lived something under a hundred thousand instead of a million years ago, at a time, that is to say, when true men were already appearing in Britain; he is indeed to be regarded, in the words of Dr Kenneth Oakley, as 'a late specialized hominid which evolved in comparative isolation.' Swanscombe Man, on the other hand, whose skull was unearthed from one of the Thames gravel terraces at Swanscombe in Kent, has triumphantly passed the fluorine test and can be assigned to the earlier part of the old Stone Age.

The earliest of the more spectacular prehistoric monuments of the southeast is Kit's Coty House with its associated stones on the North Downs, near Aylesford, Kent. This was a long barrow, but the mound with its burial chambers has long been ploughed away, leaving only an outline which may still be discerned from the air. The huge tripod of unhewn stones which remains is a dummy entrance, designed to confuse robbers. Close by is a collapsed group of stones, popularly known as the Countless Stones, and probably the remains of a chambered tomb, while other stones in the neighbourhood, probably also associated with megalithic tombs, are the Coffin Stone and the White Horse Stone. On this last stone, by a doubtless quite false legendary accretion, the Jutish Hengist is said to have raised his standard. All these tombs were originally built by a neolithic people from across the North Sea some 4,500 years ago. At a somewhat later period many people of the New Stone Age were living on the South Downs in Sussex, where you will find two of their most famous sites on Trundle Hill near Goodwood racecourse, and Whitehawk Hill near Brighton racecourse. At this time there was a regular industry of mining flint for the large-scale manufacture of flint axes. The best-known mines in the south-east are on the Downs near Findon, and the most famous of all is at Cissbury Ring, in turn also an Iron Age fortress and a twentieth-century viewpoint and picnic-spot. Here deep pits were sunk in the chalk, and horizontal galleries were driven out radially to follow the seams of flint nodules. The flints were excavated with the aid of two tools, a pick made from the antlers of red deer and a shovel carved out of the shoulder-blade of ox, deer or pig. In some places, as at Harrow Hill northwest of Worthing, not only the holes made by the picks but the soot-marks from the miners' lamps can be seen on the walls and roofs of these 4,000-year-old mines.

The Sussex Downs are also strewn with Bronze and Iron Age sites, including not only the earliest dated examples of the 'Celtic' field system – on

The port of Newhaven (below) is one of the gateways of England; Lewes Castle (above) was built to guard the gap in the Downs to which Newhaven leads.

Plumpton Plain near Brighton, dating from about 1000 to 750 B.C. – but a series of great hill-forts built by a group of Gaulish invaders who arrived about 250 B.C., and the isolated Mount Caburn, two miles south-east of Lewes. This fortress was first raised about 100 B.C., was re-fortified against the Romans and then taken by them about A.D. 43. It was again strengthened against the Saxons about A.D. 300, and finally fortified once more in the reign of Stephen over 800 years later.

The Home Counties have a profusion of extant buildings and sites of the Roman era that can hardly be surpassed (except in the Lower Rhône Valley) outside Italy itself. One of the earliest is the British stronghold of Bigbury Rings, near Canterbury, which was stormed by Julius Caesar in his second invasion in 54 B.C. You can climb the massive ramparts and scramble into the defensive ditch over which the Seventh Legion advanced with uplifted shields, as recorded in *De Bello Gallico*. Some ramparts also survive at Wheathampstead in Hertfordshire, the capital of the Catuvellauni, which Caesar went on to storm after crossing the Thames. Roman remains include the pharos or lighthouse within the castle at Dover; the *villa* or farming estate sites at Bignor in Sussex and at Folkestone and Lullingstone in Kent (at Lullingstone a fine pavement was discovered in 1949 and a flight of red-tiled steps with slabs a foot wide in 1950); the extensive remains of Verulamium at St Albans, in Hertfordshire, with its walls and theatre; and numerous portions of the walls and other buildings in London, Canterbury and Chichester. The bombing of London and Canterbury laid bare many sites of great interest, which are now being hastily explored before buildings hide them again. In London a Roman fort dating from about A.D. 70-80, not long after the city had been sacked by Queen Boudicca, or Boadicea, was discovered only in 1950 in the north-west corner of the old city wall, close to Cripplegate church.

THE OUTER WALLS OF LONDON

When Caesar, the first historical invader of Britain, landed somewhere near Deal in 55 B.C., there were no organized defences on the south-east coast of Britain, but the later coming of the Saxons was foreshadowed by the erection of a chain of forts round the coast from Brancaster in Norfolk to Porchester in Hampshire. Substantial remains of these 'forts of the Saxon shore,' as they were called, have survived in our area in Kent at Richborough and Reculver, guarding either end of the then navigable Wantsum (Thanet in those days really was an island); and even more impressively in Sussex at Pevensey, then itself an island in the marsh that is now Pevensey Level. Here in A.D. 491 there was a great slaughter of the Romano-Britons by the Saxons. At Bradwell-on-Sea, at the mouth of the Essex Blackwater, none of the Roman fort of Othona remains above ground, though some of its materials

The oasthouses and farmland of Kent.

survive in the walls of the gaunt little chapel of St Cedd, now called St Peter's
ad Murum.

It was to be 1,200 years before another chain of forts was built round the
Saxon shore. This was the medieval defence system based on the administrative device of the Cinque Ports, which some historians indeed believe to
be the lineal descendants of the Romano-British forts. The original five ports,
which gave the system its name, were Dover, Sandwich, Romney and Hythe

in Kent, and Hastings in Sussex, to which Winchelsea and Rye in Sussex were added at a later date. They all had a privileged status – which, sad to say, they abused almost to the point of piracy in latter years – in return for supplying the King with ships and men to defend the realm. Almost every other port or fishing village in Kent and Sussex, and even Brightlingsea in Essex, became a 'limb' of one of the Cinque Ports. One limb was Tenterden, now ten miles from the sea. There was a curious old belief that 'Tenterden steeple Sandwich haven hath decayed', and indeed so deeply did the burgesses of Sandwich feel themselves aggrieved by their rivals of Tenterden, that Henry VIII was constrained to set up a Royal Commission under the chairmanship of Sir Thomas More to inquire into their allegations. It now seems most probable that the excellent landmark which Tenterden steeple provided for ships navigating Romney Marsh, which was partly open water in those days, led merchants to prefer the port of Tenterden to the port of Sandwich, which was already silting up. Even to-day the Cinque Ports maintain their place in British public life, for the Lord Wardenship (the Warden's residence is Walmer Castle) is one of the great honours of state. A hundred years ago it was held by the Duke of Wellington; to-day the Lord Warden of the Cinque Ports is Winston Churchill.

In the reign of Henry III, Dover furnished the King with 21 ships, Winchelsea with ten, Hastings with six and the other Cinque Ports with five apiece. Dover is still the premier port, and is indeed the only one of the seven to remain a port in any real sense, though some of the limbs, notably Folkestone, still hold their own. Dover, in fact, remains the chief gateway to England, as it was when the Romans built both the pharos to light their ships across from Gaul and the castle to protect the port from Saxon pirates. Sandwich is now more famous for its golf links, and for having given its name to an earl who gave his name to two bits of bread on either side of jam or cucumber, than for its historic past, closely linked with the nearby fort of the Saxon shore at Richborough. Hythe, though its very name means 'harbour', is now perhaps better known for the bones stacked in the crypt of St Leonard's Church, grisly relics of the overcrowding of medieval grave-yards and perhaps also of some long-forgotten battle. The sea has retreated altogether from Old Romney, which gave way to New Romney 800 years ago, and in its turn New Romney was forsaken too, when after a violent storm in the year 1287, the Rother turned to seek the English Channel at Rye.

Rye also has been deserted by the waves, but if you come to it along the marsh road from Romney, you still get that impression of an island rising out of the sea that strikes you so forcibly in coming to Ely or Crowland across the Fens. Indeed, like the Fens, Romney Marsh is one of the esoteric regions of the south, which still has a sense of local patriotism against the rest of England. All good Men of Kent will tell you there are five continents,

Small pleasure-craft on the Middle Thames.

Europe, Asia, Africa, America – and Romney Marsh.

The Cinque Port of Winchelsea looks across Pett Level as Rye looks over the Marsh, and is just as far from the sea. Here you have a remarkable example, unfortunately never finished, of medieval rectilinear town-planning. Hastings, the western bastion of the Cinque Ports, retains its status as a fishing port in a small way, but really lives now for the holiday trade. At one time it was thick in the smuggling business, and indeed, Byron considered 'smuggling neat brandies and silk handkerchiefs' as one of the attractions of a visit to Hastings, and Lamb partook of 'smuggled Hollands' on a visit there. The Sussex newspapers during the early 1800's carried many

Barges cluster on the Thames at Chelsea.

harrowing stories of brutal affrays between the 'gentlemen' and the excise-men.

It was not until the reign of Henry VIII, in 1539, that it was thought necessary to provide fresh defences to protect the realm against the new threat of artillery attack. Of the four forts then built, the Lord Warden's official residence of Walmer Castle is the best preserved; it contains the camp-bed and other personal relics of the Duke of Wellington, who died there in 1852. At Sandgate, another of the Tudor castles is slowly being washed into the sea. The next threat was from Napoleon, and during the French wars yet another series of fortresses was built round the south-east coast. These were the famous Martello towers inspired by Pitt. The westernmost is at Seaford in Sussex, and another, known as the Wish Tower, stands on a hillock on the sea-front at Eastbourne. A few are scattered round the shore of the Marsh, where they are backed by that other fruit of Pitt's energy, the Royal Military Canal, running along the landward side of the Marsh from Hythe to Rye. Nowadays, the canal is mainly used for boating, and is known to naturalists as the place where the Continental marsh-frog has established itself in Britain, after a few specimens from Hungary were liberated some 15 years ago at Stone-in-Oxney. The latest chapter in the history of south-east England as Britain's chief area of danger and defence is fresh in everyone's mind. Instead of forts or castles, it was the forward airfields of Fighter Command, Hawkinge, Biggin Hill, Hornchurch, Kenley, Manston, which took the strain. And later, when the flying bombs began, all over the Weald there rose the silvery shapes of the barrage balloons, glossed with fire by the setting sun. They were perhaps the most curious and beautiful sight of the war.

The last occasion on which these defences of England were penetrated by an invader who came to stay was when William, Duke of Normandy, landed at Pevensey on Michaelmas Eve – September 28 – 1066. Within 16 days he had decisively defeated King Harold at the Battle of Hastings. This celebrated contest, whose date is perhaps the one fact in history known to all Englishmen, took place on an isolated hill six miles north-west of Hastings, a hill with no name except that of 'the hoar apple tree' that crowned its skyline. Historians of the last century tried to rechristen both hill and battle 'Senlac', but the name of Hastings was graven too deeply in English folk-memory for them to succeed. After his defeat and death, Harold's body was carried to Waltham Abbey in the Lea Valley, north of London, while William marched to Berkhamsted in a valley of the Chilterns which commands an important approach to London from the north-west. There he received the surrender of the nation and laid the foundations of Norman power by coming to terms with the City of London, granting the citizens their ancient rights and privileges. At Berkhamsted he began to build a castle, the remains of which are obvious to every traveller on the main railway line out of Euston, and at the south-east corner of the City of London he erected the White Tower, the keep of the Tower of London, to show the Londoners he intended to stand no nonsense. On the 'hill of the hoar apple tree' he founded Battle Abbey, with its high altar on the spot where Harold fell. What remains of the abbey is now a girls' school.

The City of London had already become a goose which laid such golden eggs that no king could afford to interfere with it too much; so for the next 700 years it remained perhaps the most important king-making institution in England. Flamboyant barons might strut in the foreground, but in the wings during any important political change were usually to be found several members of the City companies, the Mercers, the Grocers, the Goldsmiths, the Merchant Taylors and the eight other major and some three-score

The Sanctuary of Edward the Confessor and the Royal Tombs at Westminster Abbey.

minor companies or guilds. These Livery Companies attained their full development in the fourteenth century (though they originated much earlier) and from then on few significant political trends lasted any length of time that did not have at any rate the City's benevolent acquiescence. Within

40 years of the Conquest the Treasury had been removed from Saxon Winchester to Norman Westminster, and the twin cities of London and Westminster became, as they have always since remained, the political and economic capital of England. But with London as a national institution we are not here concerned, for this London, the London of the Houses of Parliament, the Bank of England, the National Gallery and the British Museum, belongs to the nation, to the Empire, indeed to the world. The London in which we are really interested is the London of the Londoners, the London that has always provided a ready market for those who till the soil of the south-eastern counties, whether they were ex-legionaries settled on the rich cornlands round St Albans, or Scots dairy-farmers who migrated south to the grasslands of southern Essex.

THE BEGINNING OF LONDON

It was the Romans who first built London, on two low gravel hills overlooking the wide tideway of the Thames at the point where the river was crossed by Watling Street, coming up from Dover and Canterbury on its way to Chester and the north. To begin with there was a ford at Westminster. Then the Romans built the first London Bridge, soon after the city was founded in A.D. 43. The two low hills were divided by the small stream of the Walbrook, which followed the course of the narrow city street with the same name, between the Mansion House and Cannon Street Station. The western hill is crowned by London's greatest glory, Wren's cathedral of St Paul. By the time the city was sacked by Queen Boudicca in A.D. 60, it could already be described by Suetonius as 'crowded with traders and a great centre of commerce', with a population of probably ten or twenty thousand. Then it was only just beginning to assert itself as a newcomer against the old tribal capitals of Camulodunum (Colchester), Verulamium (St Albans), Venta Belgarum (Winchester) and Regnum (Chichester). But the Romans made it the largest and most important town of Britain – indeed one of the largest in the northern parts of the Empire. Many centuries had to go by before it completely overshadowed all other British cities. In the Middle Ages, half a dozen other centres, Canterbury, York, Bristol, Norwich, Lincoln, or Exeter, must have regarded themselves as the equal or better of London. To-day the overwhelming fact about the geography and social life of south-east England is the dominance of London, now swelled to Greater London, with its eight million or more inhabitants, the vastest aggregation of human beings in so small a space that the world has ever seen.

In the course of its expansion, vigorously resisted by kings and governments since Tudor times, London has swallowed up not only many villages in Middlesex, Surrey, Kent and Essex, but also ancient boroughs and market towns: such as Southwark, London's southern bridgehead and starting-place of Chaucer's pilgrimage; Croydon, an outlying part of the diocese of Canterbury, with a school founded by Archbishop Whitgift, and associations with many other primates; Brentford, sometime county town of Middlesex; Kingston upon Thames, still the county town of Surrey, where you can see the stone on which Saxon kings are said to have been crowned; Bromley, the birthplace of H. G. Wells and the Bromstead of *The New Macchiavelli*; and Greenwich, from which the Royal Observatory has at last been driven by the London smoke after 300 years, but which still retains one of the finest examples of Wren's architecture in its Royal Hospital (1694). Beyond this inner ring, from which the country has retreated in much the same way as the sea has gone from Rye and Winchelsea, the advancing tide of London, to reverse the metaphor, is now lapping up to towns 15 or 20 miles from the City: Barnet on its hill, once the site of two battles in the Wars of the Roses,

The Raising of Lazarus, a Saxon relief in Chichester Cathedral.

The Norman Keep of the Tower of London, and Tower Bridge.

and now the terminal of one of London's Underground railways; Cheshunt, where old Temple Bar, the gateway designed by Wren which once blocked the traffic of Fleet Street, now stands in suburban-rustic retirement in Theobalds Park; Gravesend, where the River Thames begins to widen out into the Thames estuary; Epsom, with its horsy flavour and a fine wide High Street marred by a clock-tower commemorating Queen Victoria's Jubilee; and Uxbridge, once a famous coaching-stage on the road to Oxford but now world-famous as the R.A.F. headquarters which directed the most crucial stages of the Battle of Britain. Indeed, nearly all the towns of south-east England are now more or less tributary to London. The large seaside resorts of Brighton, Worthing, Margate and Southend subsist almost entirely on the holiday demand of the metropolis, and even Hastings, with its ancient traditions, would rapidly dwindle if no more holiday-makers were to arrive on the 'frequent fast electric trains' from Victoria. Perhaps only Dover, for centuries thriving on the cross-channel traffic, Canterbury, as the seat of the Primate of All England, Chichester, with its atmosphere of Trollope and Barsetshire on the agricultural plain beyond the downs, and Reading, now the administrative capital of the 'Southern Region', have much independence; and even Reading, 'forty minutes from Paddington', is to some extent a dormitory town.

But the towns are by no means the whole of south-east England. There is still an extensive and well-wooded agricultural countryside, from which no bowler-hatted figures emerge spruce but hurrying, to catch the 8.17 to London Bridge or Liverpool Street. You may find it, away from the main strands of the railway web, tucked into corners and pockets; around Tenterden in the eastern Weald; on the windswept marshes between the Crouch and the Blackwater in Essex, along the north Kent shore below Gravesend, and on the triune island of Sheppey, Elmley and Harty; at the foot of the downs in western Sussex, around Petworth and Midhurst, and a little farther north in the 'fold' country of the western Surrey Weald, by Alfold and Durfold, Dunsfold and Chiddingfold; in the remote north-eastern corner of Hertfordshire, between Stort and Lea; and in the valley of the Essex Roding beyond Chipping Ongar, where Beauchamp Roding adjoins Berners Roding, Abbess Roding marches with Margaret Roding, the twin villages of Willingale Spain and Willingale Doe join hands with Shellow Bowells; and White Roding, Aythorpe Roding, High Roding and Leaden Roding lie over against High Easter, Good Easter, Bacon End and Hatfield Broad Oak. In this part of Essex even the names of the houses and the smaller hamlets are a standing delight: Puttock's End – puttocks were kites – Woolard's Ash, Fitzjohns, Crab's Green, Cow Common, Boarded Barns, Thrushesbush, Abbess End and Doodle Oak.

Indeed, the true attraction of this south-eastern corner of England lies in its judicious mixture of ancient towns, some small and some large, with a patchwork of spoiled and unspoiled countryside, all overlaid with the sooty gossamer of London's pervading influence. Thanks to the three ranges of chalk hills, with their frequent gaps made by rivers past and present, many of the most interesting towns and villages either occupy strategic positions in one of the gaps, or lie along the foot of that escarpment where the chalk joins the sand and a line of springs encouraged ancient settlement. Many of these parishes have a characteristic long, narrow shape, stretching from the crest of the downs into the vale across chalk and sand and clay. Thus in the Middle Ages each community was provided with light land for pasture, heavier land for ploughing and woodland on the clay for its swine and firewood.

GAPS, TOWNS AND CASTLES

A survey of these gaps in the chalk hills, beginning at the eastern end of the South Downs, would bring you first to the magnificent Tudor castle of Herstmonceux, now the Royal Observatory's country refuge from smoky Greenwich. It has the deceptive appearance of having been built to guard the gap in the hills behind Pevensey Level, but in fact has never had a military function. The first gap through the downs is made by the River Cuckmere, and its quiet Haven is one of the few spots on the entire coastline of Sussex

St Paul's Cathedral, London.

Two medieval castles: the 13th-century Leeds, Kent (above),
and the 14th-century Bodiam, Sussex (below).

that remain unspoiled. Happily there is no motor road down to it, and if you want to cross the river at its mouth you must swim. On either side of Cuckmere Haven are the finest chalk cliffs in England, with the sole exception of the incomparable range that forms the western end of the Isle of Wight. Upstream there is no town in the Cuckmere gap. Instead, midway between the two downland ridges, stands the large village of Alfriston with its medieval inn, and the stump of the only surviving market cross in Sussex besides that at Chichester; and there is the tiny sixteen-foot-square church of Lullington across the valley, one of several which claim to be the smallest church in England, though actually it is only a chancel surviving from a larger building. The real guardian of the Cuckmere gap, however, is the Long Man of Wilmington, who 'looks naked toward the shires' from the steep northern face of Windover Hill. With a staff in each hand, the Long Man, one of the two giants carved in the English chalk (his fellow is at Cerne Abbas in Dorset), is a mystery, perhaps insoluble. There is no record of him before 1779, and it is not certain whether he is old or young, whether he is a Romano-British representation of Hercules, or even the folly of some eighteenth-century landowner. At all events he is claimed as the largest representation of the human figure in the world, standing 231 feet 6 inches high (See page 11). By comparison, the nearby horse, 66 feet high, which was cut in the downland turf above Litlington in 1924, to replace a vanished horse of the nineteenth century, is a mere pigmy.

West from the Cuckmere comes the gap through the downs made by Kipling's 'wide-bankèd Ouse', with the dull channel-port of Newhaven at its mouth; once the river flowed out at Seaford, but a great storm altered its course and created a 'new haven'. This Ouse gap is guarded by the Norman castle of Lewes, county town of Sussex, where Simon de Montfort defeated Henry III in 1264, and where the anniversary of the Gunpowder Plot is still celebrated by a riotous firework display. At the mouth of the Adur, the next Sussex river to breach the downs, the sea and shingle have played such pranks with the harbour bar that no fewer than six different openings to the sea between Shoreham and Portslade were successively used by ships at various times between 1700 and 1816. The river now reaches the sea at Shoreham, and runs back through the Downs to Bramber and the remains of its guardian castle built by the Normans. The valley here is the scene of George Moore's novel Esther Waters. Westward again is the last gap in the Sussex Downs, made by the Arun, with Littlehampton at its mouth and Arundel Castle for its fortress, one of the few medieval castles still in occupation. The Dukes of Norfolk have lived there for 370 years. From Bury Hill north of Arundel the downs curve away westwards into Hampshire, their rampart unbroken except by a few dry combes.

At Farnham, with its bishop's palace, the downs return as the high narrow ridgeway of the Hog's Back, which gives superb views north and south over the heathlands of western Surrey. At its eastern end the chalk is cut by the River Wey, and the gap, this time, is guarded by the castle at Guildford, Kingston's rival as the county town of Surrey. In full view from the main line from Waterloo to Portsmouth, you can see the new cathedral which is going up at Guildford on a low hill north-east of the town. It is only the third Anglican cathedral to be started since 1700, and indeed only the fourth since the early part of the thirteenth century. Guildford's precipitous High Street can be matched by no other town in the south-east, and by few in all England. After the Wey comes the Mole, with Dorking at one end of its gap and Leatherhead at the other, both with some pleasant Georgian architecture to leaven their garish shop-fronts and serried villadom. Here is the country of George Meredith, who lived and wrote in a cottage under the shadow of Box Hill, 'perched over yew and juniper', and of Fanny Burney, who built Camilla Lacey out of the profits of her third and worst novel, and visited General D'Arblay at Juniper Hall, where he was a prisoner of war. To-day Juniper Hall is a field study centre, thronged with keen young geographers, botanists and entomologists, and the valley, though scarred by a by-pass, still provides one of the best afternoon's walks out of London, through tall beeches and by the yews of the Druids' Grove. Reigate is the next gap town, like Dorking with relics of a pleasant eighteenth-century atmosphere, but the gap which it guards is a dry one, for no river flows northward through the valley to Coulsdon and Croydon, though a 'bourne' stream appears in very wet years. Eastward again is the Darent, the Kentish river between high hills which winds through the miraculously uncontaminated village of Shoreham, through that 'Valley of Vision' where Samuel Palmer lived and painted in the 1820's and 1830's. The Medway is the easternmost of the rivers that cross the North Downs, with Maidstone, county town of Kent, for its gap town, and at its mouth the triple town of Rochester, with its cathedral and Norman keep guarding the crossing of Watling Street over the river, and naval Chatham, and Gillingham, the largest and least distinguished of the three.

The Thames has its own gap, where it cuts the chalk between the Berkshire Downs and the Chiltern Hills in the neighbourhood of Streatley and Goring. The first town of any size below this gap is Reading, noted perhaps more for its manufacture of biscuits and its seedsmen's nurseries than for its siege during the Civil War or its unhappy association with Oscar Wilde, which made him write his one great poem – The Ballad of Reading Gaol. North-eastwards along the Chiltern scarp the first gap in the hills is at Princes Risborough, a dry valley which after a few miles produces the small River Wye, from which High Wycombe and West Wycombe take their names. As the Cuckmere may be said to be guarded by the Long Man, so the

Risborough gap is guarded by the two white crosses of Bledlow and Whiteleaf, carved in the hill slopes on either side of it. The Bledlow Cross is known to have been made in the eighteenth century, but the Whiteleaf Cross is as much an archaeological mystery as the Long Man. North-eastwards again are two dry gaps, guarded by Wendover and Tring respectively, which a few miles lower down become the valleys of the small rivers Misbourne and Bulbourne. The Tring gap is used by both the Grand Union Canal and the main railway line from London to Manchester and Glasgow, and even 900 years ago it was important enough to be guarded by the castle which William the Conqueror erected at Berkhamsted. The River Lea hardly breaks the Chiltern escarpment at the point where it rises near Dunstable; but just before it joins the Stort, it passes through Hertford, which was one of the seven towns of the Danelaw, a reminder that on this side of the Thames there was a defence problem quite different from that of the south-east coast. The valley of the Roding, though it cannot be said to breach the low hills of Essex, was in fact guarded by the Norman castle at Chipping Ongar, built by the Conqueror at the same time as Berkhamsted.

THE SEASIDE TOWNS

Beside the gap towns the majority of the seaside towns are the merest upstarts. None of the holiday resorts of our district started, like Bournemouth farther west, from nothing at all only 130 years ago; but many of the largest, such as Brighton, Southend, Eastbourne and Worthing, had very small beginnings in the reign of George III. In some the curious phenomenon of a more respectable 'West End' has grown up, and there are people who live in these superior localities who will go to great pains to impress upon you that they live *there* and not at the eastern end they suppose to be socially inferior. Thus Southend has Westcliff on Sea, Margate has Westgate on Sea and Brighton, though one says it with some trepidation, has its respectable Hove. I was at school with a boy who lived at Hove, and such was his emphasis on the fact that he lived in the 'non-trippery' town of the two, that he earned himself the nickname of 'Tripper'. But trippers or no, Brighton surpasses Hove for architecture, dating from the days when it was ultra-fashionable as the Prince Regent's favourite resort. Its Regency terraces form in fact one of the half-dozen really satisfying architectural unities in England, surpassed in the south-east only by the Regent's Park terraces in London and approached only by Tunbridge Wells and by some small corners of Hastings and some very small corners of Worthing. What is more, Brighton has in the Prince Regent's royal pavilion an extravaganza, 'Indian' outside, inside a triumph of the *goût chinois*, which is like no other building in England except Sezincote in the Cotswolds. Hazlitt had an unkind phrase for the pavilion, that it looked as if St Paul's had come down to the sea and pupped. But it re-

The stairway of Hatfield House, a great Jacobean mansion in Hertfordshire.

Jordans, the Quaker Meeting-House.

mains our most winning piece of romantic exoticism (see page 43).

Though the Home Counties can show gap towns and seaside towns, cathedral cities and even, in Reading, a university town, they are no more like London than a miniature is like a fresco. As a Londoner, I now find it hard to visualize the predicament of one who comes to London for the first time. I know its maze of streets as the forester knows his woodland tracks, but it has taken me half a lifetime to reach that pitch of familiarity. What can one advise the newcomer to do and see in that great human ant-hill, Cobbett's Wen, Dunbar's 'Flower of Cities', the much-abused yet much-loved London? The West End he is bound to see, but there for the most part lies the ugliest of London, some of the worst architecture in Britain, bad not so much absolutely but because those who paid for it could have afforded something much better. Much good building has been superseded by poor building, of which the classic examples are the Adelphi of the Adam brothers, destroyed to make room for offices before the war, and the romantic Regent Street of John Nash, pulled down and replaced with grandiose vulgarity. Waterloo Bridge is in a better state, for there, though a thing of beauty was destroyed, a thing of beauty has risen in its stead. But there are plenty of choice things left, even in the West End, such as the galleries which Nash built for the Royal Society of British Artists in Suffolk Street, or the long bland façade of Nash's Carlton House Terrace, or the Athenaeum, the club of men of letters, scholarship and science, which was built by Decimus Burton in 1829–1830, or Burlington Arcade (1818–1819) off Piccadilly, damaged by bombs but still the most elegant and select of shopping alleys, or Park Lane, where several gay-fronted Regency houses still overlook Hyde Park; and there are pleasant and unexpected nooks and corners such as the eighteenth-century Shepherd's Market tucked into Mayfair. Rebuilding has not spoilt the pleasances of the West End squares such as St James's Square, where William III is perched under the tall plane trees. The squares are each a welcome opening in the closeness of the streets, but it is pleasant to emerge now and again or to climb to points from which you have wide views of Central London – to stand on Westminster Bridge for a vista which is still splendid, though so different now from when Wordsworth saw

> 'Ships, towers, domes, theatres and temples lie
> Open unto the fields and to the sky;
> All bright and glittering in the smokeless air;'

to stand on the bridge over the lake in St James's Park for the view of the Foreign Office, or to climb the campanile of Westminster Cathedral for the vast panorama. And walk down the long vista of the Strand for the beauty of the church of St Mary-le-Strand (built by James Gibbs early in the eighteenth century), framed in the tawdry buildings from the west.

Some of the most excellent things in London can be found in the inner core immediately surrounding the West End, in Bloomsbury, St Marylebone and the City. There is Bedford Square, an architectural unity of the last quarter of the eighteenth century, happily saved from the brisk efficiency of London Transport, who wanted to thread trolley-bus wires all round it. There is St Paul's to be stalked scenically from every unexpected angle – across wastes of bomb rubble yellow with ragwort and incarnadined by rose-bay willow-herb, or down the narrow canyon of Fleet Street, the cathedral rising dim in the December dusk across the low valley of the Fleet, still flowing underground below Ludgate Circus; or St Paul's as you come in by train from New Cross Gate to London Bridge on an embankment raised above the roofs of Bermondsey. It is this railway view which shows you the cathedral Wren conceived, as it could be seen from the fields 200 years ago, set in its forest of companion spires. I recommend, too, in the stony waste of London those glimpses of green – the green of the Hampstead heights – at the far end of every turning north of Oxford Street. It was the sight of them which made the forlorn De Quincey so homesick. And you must go to the pathetic remnant of Park Village East, part of John Nash's design of Regent's Park, tattered by bombing, but still a pleasance; to the cool shades of Campden Hill, and to St John's Wood where lilac, laburnum and Japanese

32

The Londoner's character – his steadiness, humour, independence and attitude to authority – has had a world-wide influence, and has played its part in history. His loyalty to the ruler he approves is unbounded, and he likes to show it on Royal occasions.

A world as well as an empire capital, London welcomes strangers
of all countries and all colours, whether they seek refuge as exiles,
come to work or come to play. It was a popular victory when
the West Indian cricketers beat England at the Oval in 1950.

Trade, industry, finance, politics, administration – every day these bring into London a horde of black-coated workers who have their homes all over the neighbouring counties. They pour to work out of the trains and buses and across the bridges.

The Romans found access to London obstructed by the ancient oak forest of the Weald, across which they built Stane Street, leading to the harbour at Chichester. Here, in Bosham Church, Harold prayed before setting out on the journey which was the prelude to the Norman invasion.

Down the Thames London has a sea-gate in the grand style: Greenwich was a favourite Royal residence as early as 1300. The superb palace of the seventeenth century, designed partly by Inigo Jones, partly by Wren, became a naval hospital and is now the Royal Naval College. Here, too, is housed the National Maritime Museum.

London's connections with the Home Counties are mani-
fold. They include various traditional outings; a regular
one every year – an outing with pay for whole families
of poorer people – is afforded by the hop-picking in Kent.

A very different outing is the Fourth of June at Eton, when
the school celebrates the birthday of George III in one of
the loveliest weeks of the year. After the speech-day cere-
monies comes the procession of boats on the Thames.

Dover, the Roman *Dubris*, and London are connected by the old highway of Watling Street. At Dover the Romans built one of their forts of the Saxon Shore. The Norman castle and the modern naval harbour show how important this 'Key of England' has been through the centuries.

cherries adorn both the dull suburban streets and the stuccoed Regency villas. Such villas, graceful and intimate, survive in many districts three or four miles from the centre of London, in Downshire Hill and Keats Grove in Hampstead (one of the Keats Grove villas, in which Keats wrote *Endymion*, the *Ode to a Nightingale* and *Hyperion*, is now a museum filled with his manuscripts and relics), in North Hill, Highgate, in Maida Vale, Lee Road in Blackheath, or Brixton Hill. Highgate seems to keep its village atmosphere better than any of the other villages – even Blackheath – which have been swallowed up in London. A sixpenny bus ride into the outer suburbs may seem a ride into deserts empty of aesthetic delight. But how much there is to be seen! Greenwich. And not only Wren's Greenwich Hospital, with the Painted Hall, the chapel and the Maritime Museum, but the panorama over the Isle of Dogs and East London from that park which Le Nôtre designed for Charles II. Hammersmith, at the other end of London, with the houses of the Mall along the Thames, where William Morris lived and printed the books of the Kelmscott Press. Chiswick Mall, and the osier-crowned Chiswick Eyot in the river. Putney, for the Heath which runs insensibly into Wimbledon Common and is separated only by a road and a wall from Richmond Park, the three together making the finest stretch of open space so near to London. Eltham, for the remains of London's least-known royal palace; and the immediate surroundings – only – of Clapham Parish Church (1776), which have an eighteenth-century atmosphere of rest. One could indeed go on almost indefinitely writing of the odd corners of London that stick in the mind when once discovered: of the little-known Chelsea Physic Garden; of the Regent's Canal where it reappears beyond Maida Vale and runs through tree-lined streets to St Mary's Basin behind Paddington Station; of the relics of Georgian squares and terraces in Highbury and Canonbury; of the fresh, near-salty air that blows down the East India Dock Road; of the green stretch of Hackney Marshes where East Anglia points a finger into London. But there are two experiences that stick in my mind above all: the strikingly unfamiliar views of London you get from the steamers that ply between Westminster and Greenwich, and the incredible panorama from the windows of a flat on top of Highgate Hill, with the whole of London at your feet and a skyline stretching from Epping Forest in the east, along the whole crest of the North Downs from the Medway to the Hog's Back, and even, on a very clear day, to Hindhead in the far south-west, 40 miles away. Something of this view you can get from the higher parts of Hampstead Heath.

In a brief portrait such as this there would be no point, as I have suggested, in mentioning all the world-famous buildings of London and the south-east from Westminster Abbey to Canterbury Cathedral, all the great mansions from the few which survive in London such as Apsley House (which was

Above: Herne Bay, a popular holiday resort for Londoners.

Right: The Royal Pavilion at Brighton, built in an Oriental style by Nash as a holiday resort for the Prince Regent (See page 29).

given by the nation to the Duke of Wellington) to the princely extents of Knole near Sevenoaks, Hatfield House in Hertfordshire or Petworth House in Sussex, where Lord Egremont gave hospitality to Turner and Constable, and where many of Turner's finest paintings remain. Everyone can find his own way to the British Museum, the National Gallery, and the other great galleries and museums of the capital, to Milton's Cottage at Chalfont St Giles, or the burial ground of the old Quaker meeting-house at Jordans where William Penn is buried. But there are still a host of things which might easily be missed. In London, for example, you should visit, if your tastes incline that way, the scores of art exhibitions in the small galleries of Old and New Bond Street, and the streets which open off them; and it would never do

to overlook the solemn splendour of St Bartholomew's the Great in Smithfield, where in the gloom of a winter's afternoon it is easy to imagine there may be a cowled figure round the next solid Norman pier. Go out, too, into Essex for a contrast to the great churches of London in the *wooden* church at Greensted – a Saxon church, generally believed to be the one in which the body of the martyred St Edmund lay in 979; and to the round church, Romanesque once more, of Little Maplestead in the same neglected county; or go to Chaldon in Surrey, where a medieval wall-painting (see page 83) in the church depicts the terrors of the hereafter, St Michael weighing souls in the balance while a demon leans heavily on the scales and rampant devils pitchfork the bad souls into hell.

The tentacles which London is extending haphazard over the country-side.

After you have had your fill of London museums (not omitting the Soane Museum in Lincoln's Inn Fields – the private house of Sir John Soane the architect, filled with his collections, everything from an Egyptian sarcophagus and a monk's cell and catacombs to pictures by Hogarth, all evocative of the queer blends of eighteenth- and nineteenth-century tastes, of the romantic and the neo-classical, in the Waterloo era), try some of the queer little institutions tucked into odd corners of the Home Counties. If you are a connoisseur of Victoriana you may enjoy at Compton near Guildford, under the shadow of the Hog's Back, the gallery filled with the work of the once greatly-reputed artist, G. F. Watts. Another facet of the Victorian mind is grotesquely illustrated in perhaps the queerest museum in England, opposite Bramber Castle, inland from Shoreham-by-Sea. It is a museum of oddities – a hen with four legs, a lamb with two heads, dried flowers from the grave of Charles Dickens, the eleven canaries which were killed when Lady Winchelsea's favourite dog got into their aviary. Best of all are the *tableaux* of stuffed animals, 'The Kitten's Tea and Croquet Party', or others illustrating nursery rhymes such as 'Who Killed Cock Robin?' It is a museum which could only have been created in an age which knew Grandville, Lewis Carroll and Edward Lear. And then there are the butterfly farm at Bexley in the south-eastern suburbs of London, and the silkworm farm at Lullingstone in Kent, not to mention the men with a full-time job of collecting frogs to feed the snakes at the London Zoo.

Planned building: a street in Welwyn Garden City

THE MAKING OF THINGS

The great conglomerate of London means industry, in London itself and scattered about in many parts of south-eastern England. Its still somewhat grimy activities contrast sometimes jarringly, sometimes smoothly, with the traditional pursuit of farming and the quiet orderliness of the outer suburbs. The growth of London is a self-reproducing mechanism which, it seems, has not yet found its equilibrium. The industries of Slough, Dagenham and the Great West Road, drawing semi-finished light metals from the Midlands and distributing their goods and services by road to the metropolitan market at their elbow, are dependent on the high purchasing power of the great city with its millions employed in trade and administration; and in turn they add to the attractive power of London, 'the common destination of your country youths who sally forth to try their fortune' in our own day as in Miss Mitford's. To retain the vigour of this industrial enterprise, and at the same time to stop the entire London Basin becoming a desert of bricks and mortar interspersed only with parks and playing fields, calls for the subtlest integration of the demands of industry and amenity, an integration essayed with remarkable success by Sir Patrick Abercrombie in his twin plans for the County of London and Greater London.

There is little specialization of industry left in the towns of the south-east, as, for instance, in Northamptonshire, where many towns are still almost wholly given over to footwear. High Wycombe has its furniture industry, which

45

originated in the plentiful supply of timber from the Chiltern beechwoods, and the North Kent littoral is noted for its paper mills, but far more frequent is the one big factory which dominates a town or district, such as Huntley and Palmers which makes Reading known for its biscuits, or the Ford works at Dagenham, or the Courtauld rayon factory at Braintree. The Thames has lost its shipbuilding industry to the Tyne and the Clyde, though there are still small shipbuilders round the coast, at Littlehampton, for instance. Buildings and more buildings call for gravel and cement, and the only widespread extractive industries are gravel-digging, which has pitted the Thames and Lea Valleys with new lagoons (also adding at least one bird, the little ringed plover, to the region's avifauna), and chalk-quarrying for lime and cement. This has scarred the chalk escarpments with great gashes of white which (if you can see them with unprejudiced eyes) are not wholly unbeautiful. The digging of chalk for lime in an earlier age produced the remarkable caves at Chislehurst in north-west Kent, and the many dene-holes in the same district, some of them a hundred feet deep. Similar caverns used to exist under Blackheath, and there are also caves in the sandy formations in various parts of the region, as at Hastings and Godstone, most of them old mineral workings which are now known chiefly to naturalists as good places for bats. One surprise is the exploitation at Heathfield in Sussex of natural methane gas, where it was used until quite recently to light the railway station. The modern coalfield of East Kent is the only one within 90 miles of London.

One great industry has disappeared. Nowadays the Weald is one of the least industrial parts of England, a region of wood and valley and 'dim, blue goodness'. Three hundred years ago the iron-mines made it the headquarters of the nation's heavy industry. The Wealden ironstone was worked by the Romans and even before them, and on through the Middle Ages; the last forge went out of business at Ashburnham in 1828. The sixteenth and seventeenth centuries were the heyday of the Sussex ironmasters, and scattered relics remind us of the time when English naval power depended on Sussex (as well as the Forest of Dean) for its guns, and when the Wealden iron went to make the railings round St Paul's. Hammer-ponds, in which streams were dammed up to work the forge hammers by means of a water-wheel, still exist; there are two good examples on the southern edge of St Leonard's Forest; and the watercress beds at Abinger Hammer in Surrey are formed from the pond of what was once the most northerly forge in the Weald. Many cinder-beds, the ancient slag-heaps, are still to be found (the smelting fuel was charcoal from the Wealden forest), and so are many old mine-pits, and the foundations of the old ironworks, as at Minepit Copse, near Fernhurst.

THE GREAT HIGHWAYS

London has always made the south-east a region of highways, along which

46

men and horses, waggons and motors, have hurried between London and the Channel ports, a region of canals and of an intricate railway system. Before the coming of the Romans there were two great tribal roads under the shadow of the chalk hills: the Icknield Way, taking its name from Boudicca's tribe of the Iceni, but in fact much older, along the foot of the Chilterns, and the road which we now call the Pilgrims' Way, running along the foot of the North Downs. The Icknield Way is part of a great prehistoric highway right across the country, beginning with Peddar's Way in North Norfolk, continuing south of the Thames as the Ridge Way of the Berkshire and Wiltshire Downs, and reaching the sea again at Lyme Bay in Dorset. The Pilgrims' Way is part of a very ancient trackway linking the head of Southampton Water and Wiltshire with the Dover region. The Romans have left us two roads with names, and many others that are nameless; Watling Street, which still carries the Dover Road into London and the road to Chester out of it, and Stane Street, which is largely sunk in the mire of the Weald, though several fine stretches remain, including the first few miles out of Chichester towards London and most of the way from Ockley to Pulborough. To-day, when all important English roads have their official number, six of those radiating from London are graced with names as well: the Great North Road to York and Edinburgh, the Dover Road, the Brighton Road, the Portsmouth Road, the Bath Road and Watling Street, to Holyhead. They are the tentacles of a capital city, its industry and its authority. The grandiloquently named Great West Road is really only a by-pass to the Bath Road, cutting out the ancient coaching stages of Hounslow and Colnbrook.

Two scraps of railway history are worth a mention. One of the first rail-ways in all England was the now long-forgotten Grand Surrey Iron Railway, which was built between 1801 and 1805 for horse-drawn traffic between Wandsworth and Merstham. There are still traces of it by the main road in the dry valley south from Croydon to Reigate, and the present electric line from Mitcham to Croydon uses its old track. Another railway to Croydon, the one from London Bridge, uses the bed of an equally long-forgotten canal, the Grand Surrey Canal – Surrey, now rich and residential, seems to have had ideas *au dessus de sa gare* in those days – small portions of which, full of water, are visible even now around New Cross. The main canal linking London with the industrial north, still in use and now called the Grand Union Canal, has unwittingly given much pleasure to London bird-watchers, for its storage reservoirs at Hendon – commonly known as the Welsh Harp from its shape – Aldenham, Ruislip and Tring have become favourite halting places for waders and waterfowl on migration.

But before the canals there were the rivers, and indeed no Thames would have meant no London. It is the Thames which is most worth your explora-

Poultry farming among fruit trees, Surrey.

tion. It is little used now for commerce above the London bridges, and its towpath is expected soon to become one of the first long-distance trackways for ramblers. The names of the towns and villages of the middle Thames, Wargrave, Sonning, Shiplake, Henley, Marlow, Cookham, Bourne End, Maidenhead, Taplow, are all suggestive to Londoners of cool, shady willows on blazing August afternoons – or damp, dripping willows on grey, wet August afternoons, according to the luck of the weather. Lower down, the river flows through and past many places of the greatest historic interest, Windsor and Eton, Runnymede, Hampton Court, Twickenham (where Pope is buried in the parish church and where his famous grotto still exists in the grounds of Pope's villa), Syon House, Kew Gardens, whose exotic waterfowl sometimes stray on to the tideway to baffle the bird-watcher, and the charming waterside village of Strand-on-the-Green.

Of the many smaller rivers that flow into the Thames, the one with the most remarkable habits is the Mole, which, at Mickleham, is liable to disappear underground altogether in a dry season, as Spenser noted in the *Faerie Queene*:

> 'And Mole, that like a nousling mole doth make
> His way under ground, till Thames he overtake.'

The subterranean fissures in which the river travels may be quite sizeable. In 1940, for instance, a fully-grown oak tree collapsed into a hole about ten yards across within a few minutes, and on the next day the topmost twigs could just be seen in the hole about fifteen feet below the level of the ground. The Mole was once an excellent trout-stream, but like most other streams in our region, its waters have been sullied by habitation or the washings from modern roads; and few trout remain. The Thames, too, was once noted as a salmon-river, and at one time the polar bears in the royal collection at the Tower of London used to be let out into the river on collars and chains to fish for themselves. Alas, the last salmon in the polluted Thames was caught in 1833. The Thames eel-fishery survived longer, but now there is only its memory in Eel-Pie Island at Twickenham. Down the estuary, cockles are still gathered at Leigh on Sea, where you can see great mounds of their discarded shells.

SURREY FOWLS

As for farming in the south-eastern counties, it is linked essentially with the London market, and has been so for many hundreds of years. So milk, poultry, eggs and fruit bulk somewhat larger than in more rural districts such as East Anglia and the West of England. Dairying is now the mainstay of farming throughout the region, though it is concentrated especially in some areas, such as south Essex, and the hinterlands of the larger seaside resorts. Sixty or seventy years ago much of London's milk was produced in insanitary cowhouses inside the urban limits, and as late as 1905 it was possible to buy a glass of milk straight from the cow, milked by a dairy-maid in St James's Park. But an epidemic – luckily as we may think – swept off most of the town cows.

Surrey and Sussex have long been famous for their production of eggs and poultry. The centre of the table poultry industry is Heathfield in Sussex, and most of the famous 'Surrey fowls' are in fact reared in the sister county. Before the war the fowls were reared on small farms in the Weald and collected for fattening by the crammers. The processes from then on were industrial rather than agricultural. The birds were artificially fed. An indiarubber tube was inserted into their mouths and a mixture of ground oats, fat and milk was pumped into them.

There are many specialized market-garden areas in the Home Counties, but it is a sad fact that the advance of London has smothered with bricks and mortar or dug away for the sake of the gravel underneath some of the richest soil in England. In the eighteenth century market gardens covered much of the land now occupied by the boroughs of Chelsea, Fulham and Hammer-smith, and in the Thames Valley to-day the gravel-diggers will give £500 an acre for market-garden land which could produce excellent crops. South-west Middlesex still has many market gardens and orchards (the orchards are also a speciality of north Kent). One can only hope that the Town and Country Planning Act of 1947 has removed the incentive to sell such land to the builder and the gravel-digger and that the Ministry of Town and Country Planning will prove strong enough to prevent local authorities converting this fertile land to infertility. Several districts have their own specialities. Kent grows hops – where the hop-gardens, the poles and the twining stems make a peculiar, formal scenery. Worthing and the Lea Valley have their glasshouses, growing mushrooms, tomatoes, lettuces, grapes, cucumbers and flowers; broccoli and cauliflowers are grown in a limited area in east Kent; and the Chailey district of Sussex produces soft fruit, especially gooseberries, of a remarkable quality. Intensive manuring and drastic pruning of the local variety Leveller yields gooseberries weighing between twelve and sixteen to the pound.

Two tracts of marshland, Romney and Pevensey, are unsurpassed for their grazing. Both are marshes only in the somewhat specialized sense of eastern England – reclaimed marshes, that is to say, which still have a fairly high water-table and so are mainly used for sheep or cattle. Romney Marsh can now grow crops such as sugar beet and potatoes, and during the recent war much of it was in fact ploughed up. For many years though, it has been noted for sheep farming on a large scale, and it has given its name to a breed of long-woolled sheep which is one of the best-known in the world. In spring and summer the Marsh is densely stocked with sheep. Some of the best fattening land carries as many as 19 to the acre. But the Marsh is open and the winds cut in off the Channel, so in winter the lambs are moved inland to less bleak pastures. Since Romney Marsh is drained by an ancient and intricate system of dykes, hedges are not needed, though during droughts the sheep can escape and are liable to roam for miles. Pevensey Marsh, on the other hand, is mainly grazed with bullocks, and ranks among the finest fattening pastures in the kingdom. Pevensey Castle itself encloses within its walls some of the most famous of the fattening land.

South-East England has given several notable breeds of livestock to the world, Southdown as well as Romney Marsh sheep, Orpington and Dorking poultry; and Sussex cattle, the only beef breed native to this part of England, which used to be kept for ploughing the heavy clays of the Weald. The South-down was the key to a most efficient system of farming the thin, light soil of the downs. The sheep were in two flocks, 400 ewes and 100 to 200 tegs, and they were allowed to roam the downland by day. There they grazed down the coarser grasses and produced the wonderful smooth downland turf, which is now gradually disappearing except where rabbits, which nibble much closer, are at work. At night they were folded on arable crops, chiefly rape, and they trod fertility, in the shape of their own dung, back into the soil. But with scarcity of rural labour and higher wages the system became too expensive and is now dying out here as elsewhere on the English chalklands. Natural water is almost non-existent on the Downs, so the sheep had to rely on the 'dewpond on the height, unfed, which never fails.' The Sussex Downs are famous for these dewponds. You may see them on Ditchling Beacon and the famous landmark of Chanctonbury Ring. But do not be misled by myths that the ponds are replenished by dew (or by *Dieu*). Like all other ponds they owe their water to the rain. Their secret is no more than an impervious clay bottom. Since as much dew normally evaporates during the day as is deposited at night, there is no reason why it should collect and remain in a pond; and Dr E. G. Billham has shown that a pond 25 yards across in a district with a yearly rainfall of 35 inches – conservative for most high downland areas – and an evaporation of 18 inches, would collect 60,000 gallons. The water would last for three months if no rain fell at all and if not more than 166 gallons a day were drawn off.

PLANTS AND BIRDS

It might well be imagined that an area so much built-up and so much culti-vated as the south-east of England would have little in the way of wild life. It is not so at all; and in fact it might be claimed that no single county in the British Isles is more important to the naturalist than Kent – largely because it is so near the Continent. Seventeen of the 73 National Nature Reserves proposed in 1947 by a Government Committee with Dr Julian Huxley as chairman, lie in our area, five in Kent and four in Hertfordshire. In fact, as North-West Europe gradually recovers from the Ice Age, many animal and plant species are spreading north and west, and the south-eastern counties are the natural point of arrival for those immigrating into the British Isles.

In prehistoric and early historic times almost the whole of south-east England was covered with woodland. Constant felling for fuel and timber, and clearance for farming and building, have greatly reduced the wooded area, but to a much smaller extent – surprising as it may seem – than over most of the British Isles. The remaining woodland is mainly oak and beech, with some small areas of birch, pine and other trees. There are two types of oak in Britain, with and without stalks or peduncles to the acorn, the pedunculate and the sessile-fruited or durmast oaks. It is the pedunculate oak which dominates the bulk of the surviving woodland in the region, sometimes as pure oak wood, but on limey soils usually with an admixture of ash, on sandy soils often with a good deal of birch, and almost always with a shrub layer of hazel. There are extensive oak woods on the clay of the Weald and smaller woods on the gravel-capped summits of the North Downs. Between Ruislip and Harefield in north-west Middlesex are three remnants of the forest whose robbers and wolves once formed the principal hazards of a journey from London to St Albans – Park Wood, Copse Wood and Bayhurst Wood, now part of London's Green Belt. The durmast oak is found chiefly in parts of Essex, Hertfordshire and north-east Kent, where it is accompanied by the hornbeam, a comparatively recent invader which here reaches its north-westernmost natural limit in Europe. The hornbeams of Epping Forest were polled for centuries by the commoners for firewood and now present a curiously wizened look as though they were grown for witches' brooms. William Morris had Epping Forest in mind when he wrote *Shameful Death* about the knight who was murdered

'In a place where the hornbeams grow,
A path right hard to find
For the hornbeam boughs swing so
That the twilight makes it blind.'

The oak woods of the south of England are notable for their fine display of spring flowers, especially primroses, wood anemones and bluebells. A bluebell wood in May is one of the especial sights of England, and there is an excellent one no farther from Piccadilly Circus than the Queen's Cottage grounds at Kew Gardens.

The beech, which like the hornbeam is a late post-glacial arrival in Britain – but not so late that Caesar could not have seen it – is found mainly on the chalk hills, but sometimes also on sandy soils, as at Burnham Beeches, Ken

Wood and Epping Forest. The very finest beech woods in England are on the Chilterns between Wendover and Watlington (where the wild cherries make so beautiful a splash of white in the spring to offset the pale green of the young beech leaves), on the South Downs near Arundel, and on the North Downs in Surrey; and though the ground flora of beech woods is always sparse, you may be lucky enough to find the remarkable parasitic bird's-nest orchid. Their bird life is sparse as well. Yew and box are also characteristic trees of the chalk, together with the juniper, which forms scrub on the South Downs. The yew wood at Kingley Vale near Chichester, which has been described as the finest in Europe, is one of the proposed national nature reserves. Box forms woodland very locally on the North Downs and the Chilterns, notably at Box Hill, the famous view-point over the Weald only 20 miles from London. There the box trees spread from the summit down to the dark waters of the Mole which runs – or creeps – under the hill. The only extensive pine woods are forestry plantations, but much self-sown pine grows on heathlands along with birch, as for instance on Oxshott Heath and Esher Common in Surrey.

There are many thousands of acres of heathland in the south-east, frequently characterized by extensive tracts of heather, and sometimes by bilberry, or whortleberry, and by scattered trees. Surrey has many of the finest stretches, from Leith Hill westwards to Hindhead and Farnham, including Hurtwood, named from its whortleberries (locally known as 'hurts'), and Thursley Common, partially devastated by tank training. Another patch of heathland around Pirbright and Chobham in north-west Surrey is also much given over to the military, and many of the heaths of eastern Berkshire, though not Charles Kingsley's old stamping ground of Hartford Bridge Flats, are now planted with conifers.

Where the ancient woods have been felled in south-east England, we have all the main types of grassland – acidic grassland on the sandy soils of the heaths, neutral grassland on the clays and loams that underlie the meadow and pasture of the ordinary farms, and the basic or alkaline grassland on the chalk hills and downs. It is only the constant grazing by rabbits and sheep which prevent these grassy downland areas from reverting to woodland. The decline of sheep-farming on the downs in recent years is reflected in the increase of hawthorn – not yet 'gnarled and writhen' – and of elder scrub and tor-grass, which even rabbits will not eat. On the downs you will find many beautiful and characteristic flowers – in a few places, in spring, the purple anemone called Pasque-flower because it blooms about Easter-time – or in August the blue flowers of rampion, and the purple-blue of gentians. The chalk, and especially the Kentish chalk, is particularly rich in orchids; indeed thirty-seven species occur in the one county, which only lacks a dozen of the British orchids.

Modern industry along the Thames; the Ford Motor Works at Dagenham.

Marshland once came right up the Thames to within a few hundred yards of London Bridge, and at the beginning of the last century bitterns boomed in Bermondsey, bearded tits fluttered in the reeds by the Old Kent Road, and harriers ranged the dykes from Battersea to Deptford. Much of South London, indeed, is still below sea-level, as you may realize if you travel by rail out of London Bridge across the viaducts raised above the level of the house-roofs. To-day uncultivated marshes and bogs are among the scarcest types of natural habitat in south-east England, and there are no natural lakes in the region, though the numerous ornamental waters and reservoirs go far to make up for this lack. So also do the many rivers – apart from the Thames in its lower reaches, where civilization has killed off most of its more interesting flora and fauna, except for a few oddities such as the cultivated angelica (*Angelica archangelica*), which has established itself on the banks of the river between Kew and Mortlake.

The Home Counties are not so fortunate along their coastline. Industrial development along the Thames estuary, the many holiday towns, and such unplanned calamities as Canvey Island, Peacehaven and Bungalow Town have made the coast the least natural stretch in the British Isles. Yet there still remain some excellent examples of drained marsh and salt-marsh along the

Yacht-racing at Burnham on Crouch, Essex.

coasts of Essex, from Bradwell on Sea to Burnham on Crouch and on Foulness Island, and the coasts of north Kent, from Gravesend to Allhallows and on the isles of Grain and Sheppey; there are good sand-dunes at Sandwich, and extensive shingle-beaches at Dungeness and the Crumbles, near Eastbourne – all of them important for the naturalist.

THE WILD GARDENS OF LONDON

I have mentioned, too, the ragwort and willow-herb on the bombed areas of London around St Paul's, to which must be added many parts of the East End. These temporary 'wild gardens' have developed their own distinctive flora. The rose-bay willow-herb had greatly extended its range around London in the years before the war, until it became as much a part of the summer scene in the Chilterns, in Kent, Surrey and Sussex as bluebells are of the woodland scene in spring. By non-botanists it is often confused with the purple loosestrife of the ponds and streams. The yellow Oxford ragwort is a species with a more extraordinary past. It was brought centuries ago from the lavas of Sicily to the Botanic Gardens at Oxford. At last it escaped by way of Oxford walls to the railway, and then began to spread through the country by train, along the tracks. You can often see its winged seeds float into a carriage at one station and float out at another. But it is the bombed cities, and London, above all, which have given the ragwort its greatest triumphs of colonization. In several places among the ruins saplings of native sallow and of Chinese buddleia have grown ten or more feet high, and cherry-trees originating in office-workers' lunches and numerous Trees of Heaven (*Ailanthus*), also from China, push their way up through the miniature forests in the Temple, around St Paul's, and on the extensive open space behind Cheapside where the medieval church of St Giles, Cripplegate, is one of the few surviving landmarks. On a fragment of the Roman Wall near this church grows a large colony of pellitory-of-the-wall, which has been there for many years, and is now starting to spread over the surrounding ruins. It is only quite recently that the London Rocket, a yellow, rather undistinguished plant of the cabbage family, which grew in profusion in the ruins after the Great Fire of 1666, has been rediscovered in the ruins made by the great fires of 1940-41.

The bird-watcher is well served in the Home Counties, for they are particularly rich in the birds of woods and heaths, including such local species as the red-backed shrike, wryneck, and Dartford warbler, continental birds which seem to find continental conditions only in the south-eastern counties. Warblers and nightingales are abundant, and fine choruses can be heard within fifteen or twenty miles of London, in Epping Forest and on many of the Surrey commons. In the past thirty years two new breeding species for Britain have begun to colonize the south-east. One is the black redstart, mainly in the coastal towns and – like ragwort and willow-herb – in the bombed areas of the City of London. The other, the little ringed plover, frequents the many gravel-pits I have spoken of in the valleys of the Thames, Colne and Lea. One of the classic localities in the region for the ornithologist is Dungeness; it has breeding terns and stone-curlews, the only common gullery south of the Scottish border, and until recently one of the few colonies of the Kentish plover, now virtually extinct as a British breeding species. Dungeness is also the best place in the south-east to observe bird migration, and many rarities have been seen on the coastal strip towards Hastings. But you need not go so far for migrants. Take an early morning walk in the parks even in the centre of London, before the crowds come, and it is surprising how many migrant species you may observe. Inner London, in fact, has more attractions for the bird-watcher than might be expected. Kestrels are not uncommon, and even sparrow-hawks and peregrines occur now and again. In winter the gulls crowd to the river and the parks, and starlings by the thousand flock in to roost on the National Gallery and other famous buildings. Stand under the portico of the National Gallery at closing time. The starlings will not only be chattering in a deafening, trilling chorus overhead but blackening the sky over Trafalgar Square and rocketing down on to the

Nelson Column and the spire of St Martin's church. Two heronries exist even now within a stone's throw of London's county boundary, at Walthamstow on an island in a reservoir, and in one of the plantations in Richmond Park; herons often visit the central parks to fish in the early morning. In winter the many reservoirs in the valleys of the Thames and Lea attract thousands of duck, which are regularly watched and counted by members of the London Natural History Society and the British Trust for Ornithology. Many duck also come to the Thames at Chiswick Eyot, just above Hammersmith Bridge; more than a dozen different species were seen there in one recent year.

Several species of deer, including the fallow and the roe, inhabit the larger woods of the south-east, and there is a famous old herd of wild fallow deer in Epping Forest. Seals come to the Thames estuary and to the coast of Essex and occasionally stray upstream into London, to the general astonishment. Porpoises and dolphins also sometimes get carried up as high as Chiswick by the tide. That engaging egg-thief the red squirrel is found in numbers only in Epping Forest, but the introduced American grey squirrel is rather too common throughout the area, except in Essex east of the Roding. In the neighbourhood of Tring the Continental or fat dormouse, beloved of Roman epicures, is at large, after being released from Tring Park some years ago.

South-East England, too, is something of an entomologists' paradise, since it has a number of butterflies and moths that do not extend further north and west in Britain. One of them is a local species of skipper found in the marshes of Kent and Essex, a native only recently discovered and distinguished. Another is the continental race of the magnificent swallow-tail, which occurs almost every year in Kent, and sometimes attempts to breed there. Even the London suburbs have their specialities, such as the holly blue butterfly and the poplar grey moth. Among the wild gardens where the bombs fell the elephant hawk-moth occurs on the willow-herb, and the cinnabar-moth on the ragwort. The vapourer-moth is especially common in the West End, where its caterpillar feeds on the plane-trees in the squares.

THE NATIONAL PARK OF THE SOUTH DOWNS

Since building is scattered so far and wide in the Home Counties, it is not surprising that the Hobhouse Committee on National Parks in England and Wales, which reported in 1947, could only recommend one national park for the south-east. Its location – the South Downs – will tell you the whereabouts of the best and least spoiled scenery within reach of London. The park will stretch almost the whole length of West Sussex, from Beachy Head to the Hampshire border at Butser Hill, and beyond it to the Meon valley and Gilbert White's Selborne. In places, especially between the valleys of the Ouse and the Adur, it is only a narrow strip two or three miles wide, but nobody who knows the South Downs will question the wisdom of the Committee in recommending that they should be one of the select list of a dozen areas in England and Wales marked out for special preservation. It is always a good sign, moreover, when a stretch of country is so loved by its residents and visitors that they have formed a society devoted to its well-being. Thus the South Downs are the special care of the Society of Sussex Downsmen. It is a great pity that this, the only proposed national park within fifty miles of London and one of the only two within 120 miles, is not among the first three parks designated by the Minister of Town and Country Planning for establishment during 1950. No doubt, though, its turn will not be delayed so very long. Moreover, if the south-east is rather ill-provided with national parks, it is rich in those areas, scarcely inferior, of the reserve national parks, which the Hobhouse Committee has named 'conservation areas'. No fewer than five of these are in the region, the Chilterns, the North Downs, the Dungeness and Romney Marsh area, the Forest Ridges of the Central Weald, and the Hindhead area, extending southward to cover a large slice of the westernmost Sussex Weald. And you must add to these the smaller areas which, if all goes well, the Nature Conservancy, established in 1949, will turn into National Nature Reserves. They include such lovely places as Burnham Beeches, Epping Forest, Box Hill, Windsor Forest and the High Rocks at Tunbridge Wells.

The *territorium* of Roman London, its special sphere of interest, extended as far as the Chiltern scarp, and even today you do not get the feeling of leaving London behind till you have passed through one of the Chiltern gaps into the vale of Aylesbury. Almost everywhere in the Home Counties, except perhaps on the remote Essex marshes and in parts of the Weald of Kent, one has the sensation of the nearness of London. An advantage or a disadvantage? That depends on your attitude. Six hundred or so square miles have been blotted out by London itself. Long fingers of suburbia stretch deeper and deeper into the country. There exist Peacehaven and Canvey Island. Still, I am not sure the south-east is not still the most delectable part of a country which is not deficient in natural beauty. And many who have lived there, even if they do not think with Hilaire Belloc that 'the Midlands are sodden and unkind', will echo his feeling about the south –

> 'I light my lamp in the evening:
> My work is left behind;
> And the great hills of the South Country
> Come back into my mind.'

THE TOURS

A windmill in Kent.

IF you cannot wander through the country at full leisure, the 12 tours described below should give you the essence of town and countryside with the least expenditure of time.

They have been prepared with the aid of local experts; and each of the 12 routes offers a comfortable day by car or coach; or a journey of two or three days if you are bicycling.

The routes are based on four centres – Canterbury, Brighton, Tunbridge Wells and London. Any of the first three may equally well be chosen as a starting point for two of the first six tours; but to make reference easier they are numbered as though Canterbury had been chosen as the first centre. A map showing these will be found on the next page. The last six tours are day trips from London.

The tours are illustrated by special strip maps, somewhat after the style of road maps first made by John Ogilby (1600–1676) who called himself 'His Majesty's Cosmographer and Geographic Printer.' He produced the first comprehensive map of English roads.

The route is read from bottom to top of the page so that it can be followed as you go. The captions at the side indicate things of especial interest.

TWELVE TOURS

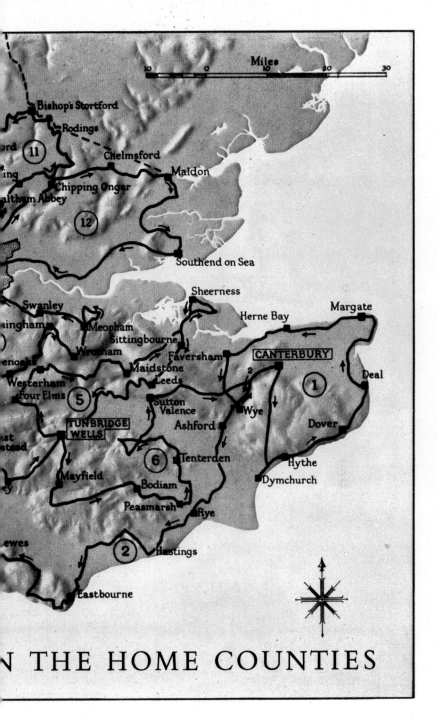

Miles

10 0 10 20 30

Bishop's Stortford
Rodings
Chelmsford
Maldon
(11)
Chipping Ongar
altham Abbey
(12)
Southend on Sea
Sheerness
Herne Bay
Margate
Swanley
ingham
Meopham
Sittingbourne
Wrotham
Faversham
CANTERBURY
Deal
enoaks
Maidstone
2
Westerham
Leeds
(1)
four Elms
(5)
Sutton
Valence
Wye
Dover
est
TUNBRIDGE
Ashford
tead
WELLS
Hythe
Mayfield
(6)
Tenterden
Dymchurch
Bodiam
Peasmarsh
Rye
ewes
(2)
Hastings
Eastbourne

N THE HOME COUNTIES

<table>
<tr><td>

Tour 1
Canterbury –
Margate –
Canterbury
104 miles

</td></tr>
</table>

Sandwich

The Royal Marines
and the Royal Naval
School of Music are at
Deal.

Dover Castle

For the next five
miles, from Botolph's
Bridge, the route fol-
lows the twisting
dykes of Romney
Marsh, bordered with
thorn bushes which
are grown specially
for sea defence.
Westenhanger Castle
on the right, once a
magnificent 14th-
century fortified
mansion.
The old Roman
'Stone Street' runs
straight for nearly ten
miles without even a
village, with views
across the valley to
the Wye Downs.

Ramsgate Harbour

At Ebbsfleet there is
a stone cross in a
meadow, marking the
reputed landing-place
of St Augustine.

Deal : Walmer Castle

Dover, nearest port
to the Continent, is
built on the site of a
Roman town.

Hythe, one of the
original Cinque Ports,
is now the terminus
of the smallest public
railway in the world.

Romney Marsh : Military Canal

Lympne, originally a
Roman fort and port,
is now a busy airport.

From the hill above
Monks Horton is seen
one of the best land-
scape views in east
Kent.

The route leaves Can-
terbury past St Law-
rence cricket ground.

From the picturesque village square of Chilham, with its old inns, and timber-framed houses, a gateway leads to Chilham Castle, built in 1616 by Inigo Jones. The route enters Canterbury at the Riding Gate, where the locomotive *Invicta*, built by Stephenson, stands.

South of Faversham, after ascending the slopes of the chalk hill, brick earth and good loam cover the chalk, providing excellent fruit-growing country, where cherries and hop gardens flourish.

On a creek of the Swale at Faversham, Jutish jewellery was unearthed. Modern industries, fruit canning and ship-fitting. The timbered Market Hall and Guild Hall are Elizabethan.

Herne Bay dates from the coming of the railway in 1833. In the village there is an interesting church with good brasses and Ruskin's 'perfect tower.'

Chilham

The watermill on the banks of the Stour at Wye is near the five-arched stone bridge, on which the names of six workmen who repaired it in 1684 are inscribed.

Kent Orchards

Whitstable, world-famous for oysters, greeted in 1830 the first passengers in England who had travelled through a tunnel by steam railway. The tunnel ran through Tyler Hill and had doors at both ends locked at night. The line was laid by George Stephenson.

Margate, once a port of embarkation for Holland, is now the most famous of all Kentish seaside towns, with fine sands and safe bathing. (Bathing machines were first used here in 1750.)

Tour 2
Canterbury –
Hastings –
Brighton
96 miles

Winchelsea, twin port and town to Rye, also occupies a defensive site on a spur of sand-stone.

Rye

Approaching Ham Street, Romney Marsh lies ahead and is reached after a short descent which marks the old coast-line here.

The centre of this part of the plain is Ashford, which grew up as a market town. It is now a rail and road junction with railway works.

At Shalmsford, concrete works use valley gravel and cement from chalk as raw materials.

The route leaves Canterbury by West Gate and follows Great Stour Valley, carved out of chalk, with steep sides and flat floor with mixed farming and orchards.

START HERE

Hastings and St Leonards have uti-lized their cliff-backed sea coast and good communications in-land to build up a prosperous seaside re-sort (*see* Gazetteer).

Pett Level

Halfway between Rye and Winchelsea are ruins of Camber Castle, originally built on a gravel bank on the seashore.

The flat, almost tree-less plain of Romney Marsh has been built up by the Eastern Rother and the sea.

Godmersham

Godmersham Park, with characteristic beechwoods of chalk country.

Canterbury: West Gate

The route passes through the old town of Lewes on a spur of chalk, with railways and roads focusing on it. The Priory lies at the foot of the spur.

Firle Beacon (712 ft.), with its long barrow, dominates this section of the South Downs.

Cuckmere Haven

Like many South Coast resorts, Eastbourne has utilized a combination of cliffs and seafront as a basis for its holiday activities. (see Gazetteer.)

Pevensey Level entered at Wartling. Like Romney Marsh, this is another area of coastal and river accumulation. Now artificially drained, it provides good grazing for sheep and cattle.

Route turns left just before Battle. The site of the battle lies just beyond the lake in the grounds of Battle Abbey.

At North Moulsecomb, the boundary between East and West Sussex is crossed and the outskirts of Brighton are entered. (see Gazetteer).

Alfriston

The route follows a steep slope down to the Cuckmere Valley.

The route zig-zags to the top of the chalk Downs and, at the last hairpin bend, gives a panorama of Eastbourne and Pevensey Level.

Pevensey Castle

The route reaches Herstmonceux Park with its castle (hidden from the road), the new home of the Royal Observatory (from Greenwich). Its removal here is to avoid smoke, electrical and other disturbances in London.

3

Tour 3
Brighton – Petersfield – Brighton
108 miles

Bosham Water Front

Bosham was once a considerable port – Harold the Saxon sailed from here on his ill-fated journey to Normandy.

The route follows a dry valley, Fairmile Bottom, with a fine beechwood on the left.

Arundel. (*see* Gazetteer.)

Mouth of the River Arun crossed by one of the few remaining toll-bridges in England.

Shoreham Bridge

Shoreham is a small port at the mouth of the River Adur. Its long associations with the sea are indicated by the ship's figure-head in the main street

Hindhead
Petworth
Petersfield
Brighton
Chichester

Mls.
Petersfield 57
Stanbridge
Compton
Funtington
Bosham
Chichester 40
Westhampnett · Goodwood
Fontwell
Climping
Arundel 27
Littlehampton 19
Rustington
Angmering on Sea
East Preston
Ferring
Goring
West Worthing
Worthing 10
Shoreham
Portslade
Brighton

START HERE

The small market town of Petersfield lies in the south-west corner of the Weald and handles the produce of the chalk, clay and sandstone districts around it.

Telegraph Hill (534 ft.) to right of Compton village, was one of several hills of the same name between London and Portsmouth from which messages were transmitted by semaphore during the Napoleonic wars.

Chichester (*see* Gazetteer).

Goodwood racecourse with the Trundle (677 ft.), which is crowned by its ancient earthworks.

Climping Church

The seaside resort of Worthing, unlike Brighton, Eastbourne and Hastings, has no cliffs.

The route leaves Brighton by the seafront. The chalk cliffs end at Black Rock, east of the Palace Pier, and the Sussex coastal plain begins here.

On a spur of the chalk, stands Lancing College (a boys' public school) with its upstanding modern chapel.

After crossing the Worthing-London road, the route passes under Chanctonbury Ring.

Stopham Bridge

The route climbs out of the Vale of Fernhurst by Henley Hill from which the Vale is seen to open out eastwards on to the Wealden clay plain where it is dominated by Black Down (918 ft.).

Just beyond Hindhead Common is the Devil's Punch Bowl, a deeply carved sandstone valley.

Hindhead, surrey

Old Shoreham, with its wooden bridge across the Adur, was originally a port but has been replaced by New Shoreham. Here the built-up area of the Brighton district begins.

Chanctonbury

Just before Pulborough, the narrow road bridge crosses the canalised River Arun which was part of the Portsmouth–London waterway before the coming of the railways.

Midhurst

Hindhead is a mass of heath and tree-covered Wealden sandstone. Deeply dissected by streams, its poor soils and steep slopes make it practically useless for agriculture. Its highest point is Gibbet Hill (895 ft, National Trust) reminder of highwaymen on the Portsmouth Road.

Between the greensand ridge and the North Downs is Holmesdale, a long narrow clay vale. Pig iron was brought here in the past to be hammered into wrought iron, hence the hammer ponds, now watercress ponds, and the well known striking clock at Abinger Hammer.

Just beyond Broadbridge Heath is Field Place where Shelley was born.

The district round Lower Beeding was once famous for iron making. The only remaining evidence of this industry are the hammer ponds just over a mile from the road.

South Downs

Brighton is rapidly growing northwards. Recent housing estates are to be seen at Patcham.

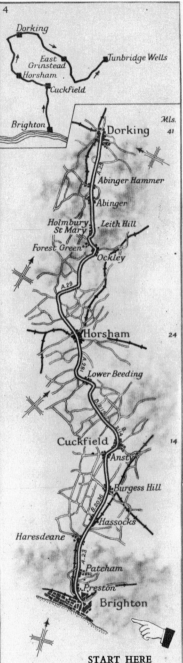

4

Dorking

East Grinstead

Tunbridge Wells

Horsham

Cuckfield

Brighton

Mls.
Dorking   41

Abinger Hammer

Abinger

Holmbury St Mary   Leith Hill

Forest Green

Ockley

A.29

Horsham   24

Lower Beeding

Cuckfield   14

Ansty

Burgess Hill

Hassocks

Haresdeane

Patcham

Preston

Brighton

START HERE

Dorking, in Holmesdale, has spread on to the sandstone country. It controls the entrance to the Mole Gap, leading to London.

Leith Hill

At Ockley the route leaves Stane Street.

The major market town of this part of the Weald is Horsham with its Carfax (cross-roads) and narrow High Street.

Hammer Pond

Cuckfield is an old market and coaching town. The railway passes it about 1½ miles to the east where Haywards Heath has grown into yet another dormitory town for London.

The route leaves Brighton at the Old Steine, and follows the London Road with the Pavilion on the left.

Eridge Park and Castle lie close to the road. On the far side of the Park is Saxonbury Hill (665 ft.) with its camp of early Iron Age. The lower slopes of the High Weald here have more fertile soils and the farming improves.

One of the finest panoramas in S.E. England is available from Marlpits – the southern slopes of the Ashdown Forest, the clay plain (Low Weald) of Sussex and the South Downs beyond, culminating in Beachy Head near Eastbourne.

The route crosses the valley of the Medway near the river's source at East Grinstead.

Another London dormitory town at Reigate. At the town centre, London Road is seen emerging from a short tunnel and the Old Town Hall is on the left of the road by the traffic lights.

Box Hill, with its patches of box and juniper bushes, is one of the favourite summits of the North Downs. It is partly National Trust property.

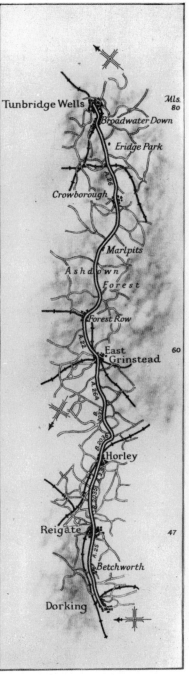

The route enters the southern outskirts of Tunbridge Wells (*see* Gazetteer).

Crowborough: Broadway

Crowborough is almost entirely a residential town.

After the steady climb from Forest Row, the route reaches one of the summits of the Forest at Wych Cross (658 ft.).

East Grinstead in the High Weald and on the main road London-Eastbourne. Busy shopping centre for the surrounding district.

From Reigate to Horley, the flattish clay plain is uninteresting. Horley lies on this plain and the abundance of timber in its old houses is a reminder of the former forest cover of this area.

On Box Hill

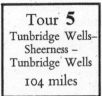

Cherry, apple and damson orchards border the roadsides until Milton is reached with its old cottages, and sweet chestnut trees which mark parish and manor boundaries. The old Court Hall dates from 1450.

Entering Maidstone, the route crosses the smooth-flowing Medway (*see* Gazetteer).

Mereworth Castle, built by Colin Campbell 1723-5, is set in extensive parkland with fine beeches and chestnuts and garden pavilions.

Knole

The route leaves the Royal Spa of Tunbridge Wells near the Pantiles, an 18th-century pavement under a colonnade with shops, and ascends the open gorse and bracken-covered Rusthall Common.

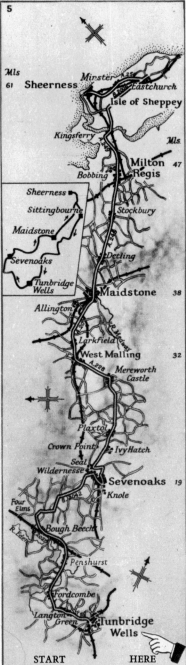

Minster

The route now descends to low flat marshland, crossing the tidal River Swale at Kingsferry, an iron girder bridge with drawbridge to allow passage for vessels into the Isle of Sheppey (the isle of sheep).

From the church at Stockbury are fine views over the Medway estuary.

West Malling: Abbey

Sevenoaks, on the lower greensand, giving it a high and healthy position, is a country market town. The High Street has charming old cottages, a fine Georgian 'White House' and a large parish church.

Tunbridge Wells: The Pantiles

Oast Houses

Loose, enveloped in hop-gardens and orchards, once had busy papermills. The old Wool House, another 15th-century timbered house, is set picturesquely on the hillside.

Otham has three exceptionally fine timbered yeomen's houses of the 15th century.

Leaving by a rowan-tree-lined road, fruit orchards encircle the villages of Tunstall and Bredgar, the route descends the North Downs.

Sittingbourne, the centre of the best cherry-growing country, is also a busy manufacturing town for paper, bricks, and cement. On the Roman Watling Street there are many interesting inns, notably the Bull, dating from 1540, and many good 18th-century houses converted into shops.

The busy main road is joined at Pembury and Tunbridge Wells is entered by the modern dignified Town Hall. (*see* Gazetteer).

Through scattered hamlets to Beltring, the heart of the hop country. Notice the white, cowled oasthouses.

Otham : Stoneacre

The main London road is crossed to Leeds, where the romantic Castle rises from the moat gleaming with water-lilies. (See page 26).

As the route leaves the island on the London clay by the only bridge at Kingsferry, Richam Docks serving the large paper mills at Kemsley can be seen, with its busy cargo ships and, on the quay, bales of wood pulp.

The dockyard and garrison at Sheerness, commanding the entrances to the Thames and Medway.

Tour 6
Tunbridge Wells – Peasmarsh – Canterbury
96 miles

Leaving Ewhurst the route follows for 2 miles a narrow twisting lane bounded by high nut hedges.

55 Etchingham

Rudyard Kipling lived at the 17th-century house, of Batemans, at Burwash. It is now a National Trust property.

Leaving Cross in Hand, ¼ mile from the inn of the same name, the route forks left to Heathfield.

Mayfield

Frant church is of especial interest to Canadians as it contains a memorial to Colonel John By, founder of the city of Ottawa.

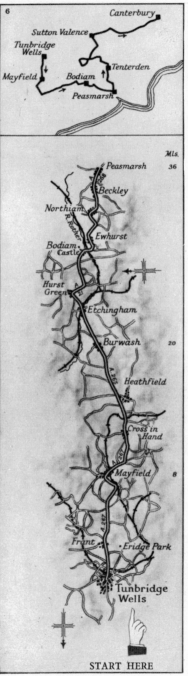

6

Canterbury
Sutton Valence
Tunbridge Wells
Tenterden
Mayfield
Bodiam
Peasmarsh

Mls.
Peasmarsh 36
Beckley
Northiam
R. Rother
Ewhurst
Bodiam Castle
Hurst Green
Etchingham
Burwash 20
Heathfield
Cross in Hand
Mayfield 8
Frant
Eridge Park
Tunbridge Wells

START HERE

Peasmarsh is a straggling village with sweet chestnut woods nearby.

At Northiam the church on the left has a 16th-century spire. The black and white timbered house on the right, 'Brickwall', is now a school.

At Bodiam visit the moated 14th-century castle, restored by Lord Curzon, and another National Trust property (*see* p. 26).

Hurst Green has many hop gardens.

Burwash: Kipling's home

Four miles on, a good view of the South Downs to the right.

Mayfield, the picturesque village, with a church dedicated to St Dunstan, has many half-timbered houses, including the Middle House Hotel, dated 1575.

In Eridge Park is the Iron Age camp of Saxonbury.

Tunbridge Wells. (*see* Gazetteer).

charing

Near Charing the large building on the hillside to the left is a sanatorium.

The road runs through Kings Wood for several miles and there is an inn in a clearing on the left with an epic name, 'Battle of Britain', recalling famous deeds of 1940 in the skies above this countryside.

Cranbrook, an old cloth weaving centre, has the tallest windmill in Kent.

Tenterden, a small Wealden town, which once had Cinque Port privileges, has several notable half-timbered houses, including the Spinning Wheel and Tudor Rose.

At Playden the road forks sharply to the left away from the coast and turns inland skirting the Walland Marsh.

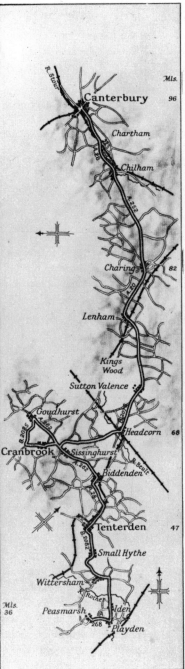

Canterbury (*see* Gazetteer).

The attractive village of Chilham has many black and white timbered houses and Chartham is on the River Stour and has local concrete and cement industries.

The North Downs can be seen on the left of the route which runs parallel to the old Pilgrims' Way on the crest of the Downs.

Lenham contains several half-timbered houses.

Headcorn now a market gardening and orchard centre, but originally connected with cloth weaving, has several 15th-century buildings.

Biddenden

Crossing the River Rother again and also the Kent Ditch (the county boundary) the road rises from the flat marches to Wittersham village on the Isle of Oxney.

Iden is predominantly agricultural, and has several oast houses.

Tour 7 London – Leatherhead– Westerham– Wrotham– Swanley– London 108 miles	LONDON –, Vauxhall Bridge – A3 – Wimbledon Common – A240 – Chessington – A250 – Epsom – Road to the Racecourse – A246 – Leatherhead – B2033 – Box Hill – Pebble Combe – B2032 – Chipstead – Chaldon – B2031 – Caterham – A22 – Godstone – A25 – Westerham – B2211 – Otford – A255 – Farningham – A20 – Wrotham – A227 – Meopham – B2000 – Cobham – A2 – Southfleet – A227 – Meopham – B260 – Sutton at Home – Swanley – A20 – Foots Cray – Lee Green – New Cross – Westminster Bridge – LONDON

For plan of route, see Tours Index map on pages 60-61.

General Description.—Through the North Downs to the Weald of Kent and fruit orchards of the south-east.

Detailed Commentary.—The route leaves London by Wimbledon Common and the Kingston By-pass, passes Chessington Zoo and the buildings where Ordnance Survey maps are produced, and turns off to Epsom, with its famous racecourse high on the North Chalk Downs where the Derby and the Oaks are run. The route then crosses the Downs and descends to the valley at Leatherhead with its ancient bridge over the River Mole. Past Tot Hill the road rises up again to the famous viewpoint and proposed nature reserve of Box Hill with its beechwoods and bluebells and steep slopes grown over with box. From here by a devious route along one of the highest parts of the Downs the village of Chaldon is reached, where the tiny church has a most remarkable doom painting (see page 83), and thence through Caterham and down to Godstone.

The route continues along the foot of the Downs, making occasional detours on to the greensand ridge to the south through Oxted, with its old market house, and Limpsfield to Westerham and where Winston Churchill has his country home, Chartwell. At Westerham, General Wolfe was born (1726). Lullingstone boasts a noted silkworm farm housed in part of the Tudor castle where the silk for Princess Elizabeth's wedding dress was produced (tours round the farm and castle). At Eynsford, just beyond Lullingstone, there is a fifteenth-century bridge over the River Darent, and Captain Bligh of the *Bounty* lived at Farningham farther along the road. From here the route turns south-east to Wrotham, near which there are glorious views from beech-covered slopes over the Medway Valley.

The route continues through Meopham on to Cobham (Kent), a historic village with its 'Leather Bottle' Inn, a church possessing a collection of medieval brasses and a sixteenth-century hall standing in a park. From Darenth – with its partly Saxon church – the route returns to London through some of the finest fruit orchards in England.

Tour **8** London – Guildford– London **96 miles**	LONDON – A303 – Wimbledon Common – A3 – Guildford – Road to Ash – A321 – Pirbright – A321 to B3015 – Bagshot Heath – Road to Surrey Hill – Road to A322 – A30 – Sunningdale – Virginia Water – A328 – Englefield Green – Runnymede – A308 – Egham – A30 – Road to Chertsey – B375 – Hampton Court – A308 – A307 – Richmond – Hammersmith Bridge – Hyde Park Corner – LONDON

For plan of route, see Tours Index map on pages 60-61.

General Description.—South-west through Surrey to the North Downs; through heath and parklands back to London along the Thames.

Detailed Commentary.—The route leaves London through Wimbledon, famous for its international lawn tennis, and passes across the first of many Surrey heaths and commons to Kingston upon Thames, county town of Surrey, with its busy market and modern shopping centre. The stone on which Saxon kings were crowned can be seen in the grounds of the Town Hall.

The road crosses Esher Common, along the Portsmouth Road to Cobham (with its fifteenth-century church) and on to the gardens of the Royal Horticultural Society at Wisley (open to the public), with its wide variety of trees and shrubs. Just beyond Guildford and its wide High Street and Jacobean Abbot's Hospital, the route crosses the River Wey and rises on to the crest of the narrow chalk ridge of the Hog's Back, from where there are fine views both to the north over the Thames Basin and to the south over the Weald (the Anglican cathedral under construction at Guildford can be seen from here).

After a detour south to the village of Seale, the route plunges across the military heathlands of west Surrey to Bagshot and then turns back up the Exeter road to Virginia Water, an artificial lake on the edge of Windsor Great Park. Here a detour is made to the meadow of Runnymede where, in 1215, King John was forced to sign Magna Charta, curtailing the royal power. From here the route returns to London through Chertsey and Hampton Court, the Tudor Palace given by Cardinal Wolsey to Henry VIII in 1526. The fine William and Mary garden façade, Mantegna cartoons, State apartments, herbaceous borders, knot garden, the Dutch garden and the Maze should be seen.

The route passes Bushy Park, with its famous horse-chestnut avenue, and climbs Richmond Hill, with the Star and Garter Home for War Wounded, overlooking Richmond Park and a magnificent bend in the Thames, and on to Mortlake, winning-post of the annual Oxford and Cambridge boat race.

Tour 9

London –
Princes
Risborough–
London

106 miles

LONDON – A403 – Uxbridge/Denham roundabout – A332 – Road to Stoke Poges – B473 – Burnham Beeches – Beaconsfield – B474 – Penn – A404 – High Wycombe – West Wycombe – A4010 – Princes Risborough – B4009 – Watlington – B480 – A423 – Henley on Thames – A4155 – Reading – A329 – Wokingham – Ascot – A332 – Windsor – Slough – A4 – Hounslow – Chiswick – LONDON

For plan of route, see Tours Index map on pages 60-61.

General Description.—The route crosses the Chiltern Hills, follows the foot of their scarp slope for a short way and then cuts back again to the Thames Valley to return to London.

Detailed Commentary.—The route leaves London by Western Avenue, passing the White City Stadium and Northolt Airport, and soon arrives in a district with many historic and literary associations. In the village of Stoke Poges Gray wrote his famous *Elegy in a Country Churchyard.* Burnham Beeches were saved for the nation by the City Corporation and a detour may be made to Jordans with its old Friends' Meeting House and Mayflower Barn, or to Chalfont St Giles to see Milton's cottage. Beaconsfield has many old houses and inns, and Edmund Burke is buried near the restored fifteenth-century church. Nearby is the village of Penn, the ancestral home of William Penn, founder of Pennsylvania.

The route descends steeply into High Wycombe, where there are some pleasant eighteenth-century houses, and passes to West Wycombe, most of which is National Trust property. West Wycombe Park is open to the public.

The route then passes between the downlands of the Chilterns to Princes Risborough (the Prime Minister's country residence, Chequers, is close by) and thence along the pre-Roman Icknield Way at the foot of the wooded Chiltern scarp visible to the left. From the old market town of Watlington it turns back through the heart of the hills to Henley on Thames, where the annual regatta is held, and crosses the Thames at Reading (famous for its beer, seeds, biscuits and cattle market).

The road passes through rich farmlands of Berkshire to Ascot racecourse, through Windsor Great Park to the castle – State apartments shown daily. See St George's Chapel, with its magnificent roof and Garter banners.

Across the river is Eton College, the public school, founded by Henry VI, and from here to London the route lies through the flat plain of the Thames basin, intensively cultivated in parts by market gardeners for the London markets and with modern factory development along the Great West Road for several miles. The great new London Airport is passed at Heathrow, and the Royal Botanical Gardens of Kew are just off the route to the right.

<table>
<tr><td>

Tour 10

London –
Welwyn –
London

95 miles

</td><td>

LONDON – Regent's Park – Watford By-pass (A500)
to Hendon – Brockley Hill – A5 to Elstree – St Albans –
A414 to Hatfield – A1 and B190 to Welwyn Garden City –
Ayot St Lawrence – B652 to Harpenden – A6 and B487 to
Redbourn – A5 to Markyate – B4540 to Whipsnade –
B489 to Ivinghoe Beacon – By-road to B4506 to Ashridge
Park – Berkhamsted – A416 to Chesham – Latimer – A404
to Rickmansworth – Pinner – Paddington – LONDON

</td></tr>
</table>

For plan of route, see Tours Index map on pages 60-61.

General Description.—Through the north-west of London suburbs, along
Watling Street to St Albans; across to Hatfield and Welwyn and on to the
crest of the Chilterns; to Whipsnade and back to London via Chess Valley.

Detailed Commentary.—The route leaves London, passing Regent's Park with
its famous Zoological Gardens, Hampstead Heath and residential suburbs
as far as Mill Hill, where there is a boys' public school. Next comes the
Elstree district with its film studios, and the route continues along Watling
Street to the first interesting town on the route, St Albans, the Roman
Verulamium, with a cathedral having Roman bricks and tiles in the fabric,
and some of the finest Roman remains in England, including an amphitheatre.

The route continues to Hatfield House (see page 30), home of the Cecil
family for over 300 years and open to the public, with its park, throughout
the summer. The house is unchanged in style since 1612 and is a very fine
example of Tudor architecture. It contains relics of Queen Elizabeth and
family portraits. The modern garden city of Welwyn, which is next passed,
provides a contrast with its factories and housing estates.

The route becomes more rural and invades the fastness to which Bernard
Shaw has retreated at Ayot St Lawrence, after which Harpenden with its
fine gorsy common and the famous Rothamstead Agricultural Research
Station is reached.

Climbing the Chiltern ridge, the route follows Watling Street again for
a few miles and then diverges to Whipsnade, with its Zoological Park,
where the animals are kept under semi-wild conditions. The route continues
to Ivinghoe Beacon, a famous Chiltern viewpoint over the Vale of Aylesbury,
to Ashridge Park, with its ancient oaks and the Bonar Law College, and on
to Berkhamsted where there are remains of a Norman castle.

The route crosses to the Chess Valley where Chesham has a partly Norman
church, Latimer has an Elizabethan mansion owned by Lord Chesham, and
Chenies has picturesque thatched cottages.

The road returns to London, passing through Harrow with its famous
school, and Wembley, with a football and sports stadium and swimming pool.

<table>
<tr><td>

Tour **11**

London –
Hertford –
London

95 miles

</td><td>

LONDON – Aldgate – A11 (Mile End Road) – Epping –
A122 to North Weald – B184 to Fyfield – By-road to
Willingale Spain – Hatfield Forest – B1005 to Bishop's
Stortford – A120 to Little Hadham – By-road to Furneux
Pelham – B1038 and B1368 to Braughing – Puckeridge –
By-road to Much Hadham – A119 to Widford – Hertford –
B158 and by-road to Bayford – By-road to Broxbourne –
B194 to Waltham Abbey – A112 to Chingford – Hackney –
LONDON

</td></tr>
</table>

For plan of route, see Tours Index map on pages 60-61.

General Description.—From the north-east suburbs of London to Epping
Forest and the Rodings, across into Hertfordshire and back into London by
the Lea Valley.

Detailed Commentary.—The route leaves the north-east suburbs through
Woodford Green, with its fine avenue of chestnuts, and on to Epping Forest.
These 6,000 acres of unspoiled woodland have been preserved by the
Corporation of London, and boasts a herd of fallow deer descended from
those hunted by the medieval kings.

Epping Town is reached and the route goes on through pleasant farmlands to the twin villages of Willingale Spain and Willingale Doe, whose
churches stand side by side in the same churchyard. Then on through three
of the eight Roding villages of mid-Essex to Hatfield Forest, remains of an
extensive stretch now under the control of the National Trust.

The route continues through Bishop's Stortford, birthplace of Cecil
Rhodes, into a little-known part of rural Hertfordshire. It turns back to the
old malting town of Ware on the River Lea, and then to the county town of
Hertford, both of which still retain many eighteenth-century buildings.
Continuing southwards past Bayfordsbury, new home of the great
horticultural research station named after John Innes, the road soon turns
east to cross the Lea again at Broxbourne.

Following the Lea Valley, with its flourishing glasshouse industry, the
route passes near Waltham Cross, where the finest of the three Eleanor
Crosses still stands. Here, too, large condensers close to factories can be seen.
To Waltham Abbey, King Harold's body was brought after the Battle of
Hastings, and the abbey church contains Norman pillars.

Passing several of London's reservoirs, Epping Forest may again be seen
on the hill to the left, with the spire of High Beech Church.

The residential suburb of Chingford is reached and then on to Waltham-
stow, which has a grammar school and almshouses, and a fine modern
Town Hall and Technical College adjoining. The route continues across the
Hackney marshes and through built-up areas to Central London.

Tour **12** London – Maldon – London 116 miles	LONDON – Aldgate – A11 (Mile End Road) – A113 – Woodford Bridge – Abridge – Chipping Ongar – A122 to High Ongar – Writtle – A414 to Danbury – By-road to Little Baddow – Maldon – B1018 to Latchington and Snoreham – B1012 to Cold Norton – Battlesbridge – A130 and A129 to Rayleigh – Southend-on-Sea – Coast road to Westcliff-on-Sea – Leigh on Sea – A13 to Hadleigh – Rainham – Barking Level – Aldgate – LONDON

For plan of route, see Tours Index map on pages 60–61.

General Description.—From the north-east suburbs of London through Roding Valley to the flats of Essex river estuaries and back along reclaimed Thames marshland to the thickly populated dock areas.

Detailed Commentary.—The route passes through the north-east suburbs of London as far as Woodford Bridge, where the open valley of the River Roding is followed for some miles. Chigwell is reached, with its interesting King's Head Inn ('The Maypole' in Charles Dickens's *Barnaby Rudge*).

Crossing the River Roding at the attractive Passingford Bridge, the road leads through arable lands to Chipping Ongar, with its Norman castle remains. Then across pleasant farmlands, to Writtle with its old houses around a wide green and its modern agricultural college, as far as Chelmsford (see Gazetteer), which has a parish-church cathedral, to Great Baddow and on to Danbury, whose 353-foot hill is one of the highest points in Essex.

Maldon (*see* Gazetteer), the next town, lies at the head of the Blackwater Estuary, with its creeks and mudflats popular with both the yachtsman and the wildfowler. Beeleigh Abbey, founded in 1180, is in an attractive setting near the head of the River Chelmer tidal waters.

A detour of about 20 miles may be made to visit the old chapel of St Peter's on the Wall, built by the Saxons on the site of a Roman fort, at Bradwell-on-Sea, and the sailing and oyster centre of Burnham on Crouch.

The route skirts the estuaries of the Crouch and Roach to reach the hill-top town of Rayleigh. Hockley and Rochford are passed on the way to Southend-on-Sea, the favourite seaside resort of London's East-enders. The pier – over a mile long – with electric trams, is said to be one of the longest in existence.

Leigh on Sea, yachting and fishing centre, famous for cockles, and Hadleigh, with a castle painted by Constable. Following the reclaimed river marshlands back to London, the route passes through the flat farmlands of South Essex, which provide much of London's milk supply, to Dagenham, with its famous housing estate and factories. At Barking, the abbey ruins contain twin fifteenth-century towers, which contrast with the two modern pylons of the electricity power station, one of the largest in Britain.

Further along, the densely populated dockland areas are reached before coming once more to Central London.

A GAZETTEER

OF

THE HOME COUNTIES

BY H.G.STOKES

NOTE

*This is a selective gazetteer of places and points of special interest or character –
a topographical anthology. The numbers show the pages on which main references
to these occur; bold type refers to illustrations.*

*For information about hotels, early closing days, markets, garages, etc.,
readers should refer to publications of the British Travel and Holidays Association,
the British Hotels and Restaurants Association, the Royal Automobile Club,
the Automobile Association or the Cyclists' Touring Club.*

*Many towns issue comprehensive lists of accommodation and guide booklets
which can be obtained from the local Information Office. Further useful advice
is also available in the area Holiday Guides published by British Railways.*

ABINGER HAMMER, Surrey.
A projecting clock, with figure of a working
blacksmith, gives an air to the village street.
Water from a nearby stream worked the hammer mill when Abinger engaged in the Wealden
iron industry. Beatrice Webb (1858-1943) is
commemorated by Beatrice Webb House, an
educational centre for residential conferences,
etc.
Dorking 4 m. N.E.

ALFRISTON, Sussex. 27.
The lion outside the *Star Inn* was a ship's figure-
head: the rest of the frontage is 16th-century.
Note roof of 14th-century priest's house
(National Trust). Alfriston church is one of the
largest among the South Down churches,
whilst across the River Cuckmere is Lullington
church, reputed the smallest in England. Ber-
wick church, 2 m. N., has modern murals.
Seaford 3½ m. S.W.

AMBERLEY, Sussex.
Village, downs and chalk-pit are familiar to pic-
ture-lovers, and the River Arun hereabouts is
good for fishing. Norman church. Imposing
remains of a castle of the Bishops of Chichester
complete with a fine manor inside.
Arundel 3 m. S.

AMERSHAM, Buckinghamshire. 9.
Here the road through the Misbourne valley
widens and is bordered by an almost unbroken
sequence of 17th- and 18th-century houses, with
a red brick Town Hall on arches.
Beaconsfield 4¼ m. S.

APPLEDORE, Kent.
A little village which looks so much larger and
more important when approached across the
Marsh from New Romney and entered by
crossing the Military Canal. Its fine church and
many picturesque houses date from its medieval
heyday as a weaving town. Rye 6 m. S.W.

ARUNDEL, *Sussex.*

The ancient castle of the Dukes of Norfolk rises above the hillside streets with their medieval buildings and rivals Windsor in its grandeur. Though the castle has Saxon and Norman work, much of its exterior facing is modern in 13th-century style. Arundel church is separated into parish church and Fitzalan chapel—the latter only accessible from the castle. The Roman Catholic church was designed by that J. A. Hansom whose name is still remembered in connection with horse-drawn cabs. In Arundel Park is Swanbourne Lake.

Littlehampton 3 m. S.

ASCOT, *Berkshire.*

The race-course is one of the best equipped and still the most fashionable in England. The race for the Gold Cup is run in June, and 'Ascot Week', is a time of festivity here, at Windsor and on the River Thames.

Windsor 5 m. N.E.

ASHRIDGE, *Hertfordshire.*

On the site of a once-famous monastery stands the great house built by Wyatt in 1808 and now used as a non-political School of Citizenship. There are good gardens (open to visitors on certain days) and the park merges into a great stretch of beechwood and downland belonging to the National Trust and including Ivinghoe Beacon (811 ft.).

Berkhamsted 3 m. S.

AYLESFORD, *Kent.*

Picturesque village with a 14th-century bridge over the River Medway and a friary incorporating remains of a 13th-century Carmelite foundation. Since 1949 it has been reoccupied by Carmelites. Less than 2 m. N.E. is the dolmen known as Kit's Coty House (page 12).

Maidstone 2¼ m. S.E.

AYOT ST LAWRENCE, *Hertfordshire.*

There is a remarkable and imposing church here with a Doric portico like a Greek temple (1778-1779), designed by Nicholas Revett. In 1944 George Bernard Shaw gave to the National Trust his house, 3½ acres of garden and the summer house in which most of his writing has been done; the whole is known as Shaw's Corner.

Harpenden 4 m. S.W.

BEACONSFIELD, *Buckinghamshire.*

The older part, with its many pleasing houses, borders the wide main street. Near the railway station is a modern residential area containing Bekonscot model railway and village. Edmund Burke (1729-97) and Edmund Waller (1606-87) lived at Beaconsfield and are buried in the churchyard.

High Wycombe 5 m. N.W.

BERKHAMSTED, *Hertfordshire.* 19.

Roadside town with considerable remains of the castle begun, but never finished, by William the Conqueror. The old rectory was the birthplace of William Cowper (1731). On a hill S. of the town is Thomas Coram School (formerly Foundling Hospital), moved here from London in 1935. Here is the organ given by Handel, and the school has a full score of *The Messiah* bequeathed by him.

Hemel Hempstead 4 m. E.

BEXHILL, *Sussex.*

About as old as the motor-car. One of the novel features of the new resort founded by Earl de la Warr was the first motor race-track in England: about half a mile long and where the parade now runs eastward from the modern pavilion (one of the notable examples of architectural modernism in Great Britain). Old Bexhill, a mile inland, is still something of a village, the hill crowned with a Norman church.

Hastings 5 m. E.

BISHOP'S STORTFORD, *Hertfordshire.*

The old vicarage in which Cecil Rhodes was born (1853) is now a Rhodes Museum. Eastward is Hatfield Forest (National Trust), an ancient deer park, with fine trees and a lake.

Epping 12 m. S.S.W.

BODIAM CASTLE, *Sussex.* **26.**

The imposing walls of the 14th-century castle rising beyond the lily-filled moat are a lovely sight. The castle was dismantled in 1643 (National Trust). Open weekdays and also on Sundays in summer.

Robertsbridge 3 m. W.S.W.

BOGNOR REGIS, *Sussex.*

'Regis' was added to the name by royal command in commemoration of George V's convalescence here in 1928. The town has since extended to include Aldwick Manor, where he stayed. Chichester 7 m. N.W.

BOSHAM, *Sussex.* **36.**

'Bozzam', as it is pronounced locally, is old enough to have figured on the Bayeux Tapestry – indeed, the remains of Canute's daughter were found in the church in 1865. Tucked away beside a creek of Chichester Habour, it is a haunt of boating men and artists. The church has a Saxon tower.

Chichester 3½ m. E.

BRAINTREE, *Essex.*

The only town in East Anglia which still maintains on any considerable scale the weaving which made it prosperous in medieval times. Ancient cloth weaving gave way to silk in the 18th century. To-day Courtaulds turn out huge quantities of rayon, while Warners make fine handloom silks and tapestries for furnishing. Another local industry is the manufacture of metal windows. Buildings are also a blend of old and new. St Michael's church tower has a cote for a sanctus bell projecting from its spire. The modern Town Hall has a museum of local relics. Chelmsford 12 miles S.W.

BRAY, *Berkshire.*
Thames-side village with a charm that fully explains the reluctance of the famous vicar to surrender his living. 15th-century lych-gate at entrance to churchyard and the mellowed brick almshouses of Jesus Hospital (17th-century). Here, too, is good food and drink for the traveller.
Maidenhead 1 m. N.

BRIGHTON AND HOVE, *Sussex.* 29, **43.**
The Prince Regent and Dr Russell between them not only founded the popularity of Brighton as a resort but established seaside holidays as an English institution – the former with the Pavilion, the latter by his insistence on the medicinal properties of sea-bathing. Brighton, moreover, boasted the first promenade pier built round our coasts. It maintains its progressive reputation, but among the multiple shops and cinemas and fun fairs is a surprising amount of good Georgian and Regency architecture. Hove (a separate borough) almost miraculously retains its Edwardian dignity, and the romantic, pseudo-oriental Pavilion designed by John Nash is a treasure house of internal decoration, furniture, pictures, etc. Brighton has some very good schools, headed by Roedean, a mile or so east. Being an hour distant from London by rail, it is a popular residential town.
Lewes 8 m. N.E.

BROADSTAIRS, *Kent.*
Sandwiched between Ramsgate and Margate, houses and hotels peer over the chalk cliffs to the sandy bay with the 'queer old pier' beloved by Dickens – who lived here for a time. It retains something of a Dickensian atmosphere.
Ramsgate 2½ m. S.

BURNHAM ON CROUCH, *Essex.* **55.**
Noted for its oyster beds and the good sailing in and beyond the River Crouch.
Shoeburyness 7 m. S.W.

BURWASH, *Sussex.*
Bateman's, the 17th-century house long the home of Rudyard Kipling, is now in care of the National Trust, and with its gardens is open on certain days.
Battle 7 m. S.E.

CAMBER CASTLE, *Sussex.*
Thanks to neglect of Charles I's order for its demolition, the castle remains one of the best examples of a coastal defence work of Henry VIII. When built (1531-9) it was close to the shore; since then the sea has receded nearly a mile. Rye 1 m. N.

CANTERBURY, *Kent.*
In the font of St Martin's church (Saxon built of Roman materials) King Ethelbert was baptised (597) by St Augustine, who founded the great cathedral. In which cathedral (Norman built on Saxon site) Becket was murdered (1170), was acclaimed a martyr, his shrine the goal of countless pilgrimages and the repository of untold wealth in jewels and ornaments. Offerings brought by the pilgrims (see Chaucer) helped to build the cathedral as we know it.
Older far than Augustine, Canterbury grew up on a natural route centre. The Dane John is an ancient earthen mound, and recent excavation on sites bombed during the war have disclosed remains of the Roman *Durovernum.* Until the Reformation made an end of the pilgrimages, it was a place of the greatest importance. The West Gate of its walls remains, and a dozen old churches and many medieval buildings testify to the vigour and variety of its life. As a modern country town it is well seen during the cricket festival in July.
Rochester 27 m. N.W.

CHALFONT ST GILES, *Buckinghamshire.*
Hither in 1665 came John Milton to escape the plague ravaging London, and here he finished *Paradise Lost* and began *Paradise Regained.* His cottage is now a museum. The church has notable wall paintings.
Amersham 3 m. N.W.

CHANCTONBURY RING, *Sussex.*
Conspicuous landmark (783 ft.) of the South Downs formed by a plantation of beech trees surrounding a small Iron Age camp. Walk by the ridgeway to the larger camp of Cissbury where the shafts of Neolithic flint mines are visible on the surface. Worthing 7 m. S.

CHARING, *Kent.*
A large village on a southern slope of the North Downs, woods above and views of the Weald below, and with an air of dignity derived from the days when its archiepiscopal palace (now ruins) entertained most of the eminent men of the day. Canterbury 13 m. N.E.

CHATHAM, *Kent.*
A naval dockyard has been here since the 15th century, and the protecting forts occupy the 'lines' fortified in the 18th century. Gillingham (pronounced 'Jillingham') to the N., was the home of Will Adams (1575-1620), the first Englishman to settle in Japan and virtual founder of Japanese sea-power. Maidstone 8 m. S.

CHELMSFORD, *Essex.*
A bare hour from London is this county town and agricultural centre (especially dairy farming). St Mary's church is now the cathedral. The Shire Hall contains good work of the Adam period. Maldon 8 m. E.

Medieval wall-painting of the Last Judgement, Chaldon (see page 43).

CHICHESTER, *Sussex.* **22.**
The exquisite 15th-century Market Cross stands at the intersection of roads planned by the builders of Roman *Regnum*, and in wall of the Council House is a Roman inscribed stone brought from Goodwood. The cathedral is mostly Transitional Norman, with a detached bell tower and two sculptures which may be Saxon. See St Mary's Hospital, St Olave's Church and the many good domestic buildings.
Portsmouth 13 m. S.W.

CHIDDINGSTONE, *Kent.*
A picturesque village of timbered houses of which the greater part is now owned by the National Trust. Hever Castle was possibly the birthplace of Anne Boleyn. Here she met Henry VIII, who subsequently gave the place to Anne of Cleves.
Tonbridge 5 m. E.

CHISLEHURST, *Kent.*
A London suburb 11 miles out. Here are the Chislehurst Caves, chalk mines (though they have not the antiquity attributed to them by guides) fascinating to explore. Circles of green light appear in the roof from the 'dene holes' – the original entrances.

CHISWICK, *Middlesex.*
Chiswick Mall, overlooking the river, is a lovely row of Georgian houses, associated with such figures as Turner, Kneller and William Morris. Hogarth lived nearby, and is buried in Chiswick churchyard. Pope and Thackeray also lived here and the neighbourhood appears in *Vanity Fair.* Whistler also lies in the new cemetery. Chiswick House (now publicly owned), designed and built after 1725 by Lord Burlington in the neo-Palladian style, is a building of the greatest historic interest which 'opened an architectural era which, it is safe to say, changed the face of England.' Kew 2½ m. W.

COBHAM, *Kent.*
The *Leather Bottle* Inn (see the *Pickwick Papers*) has Dickens relics. The church has the finest collection of brasses in England. The Elizabethan Hall stands amid lovely gardens to which visitors are admitted. Owletts (National Trust), a red brick house of Charles II's reign, is open to the public on Thurs. afternoons.
Rochester 3½ m. E.

COBHAM, *Surrey.*
The villages of Church Cobham and Street Cobham stand beside the River Mole, where is an old water-mill. See Church Stile House and (National Trust) Cedar House, a 15th-century H-shaped building with an unusual timbered roof to its great hall. (May be seen on application.) The mansion of Pain's Hill is surrounded by one of the most exquisite of English landscape gardens of the 18th century with superb trees, temples, grotto and lake filled from the Mole by a waterwheel. Epsom 6 m. E.

83

CRANBROOK, Kent.
Picturesque town owing much to Flemish weavers, who left a delightful timbered cottage and a magnificent church. The windmill is said to be one of the largest yet working in England.
Tenterden 7 m. S.E.

CROWBOROUGH, Sussex.
The Beacon (792 feet) is the highest point of Ashdown Forest. A haunt of Richard Jefferies, who lived at Downs Cottage.
Tunbridge Wells 7 m. N.E.

CROYDON, Surrey.
From a quiet town adjacent to the first London Airport, Croydon has rapidly developed into a busy industrial area. Notable old buildings include the 14th-century Archbishop's Palace (now a school) and the Whitgift Hospital (1596).
Reigate 10 m. S.W.

DEAL, Kent.
Though Deal has no harbour, it still ranks as one of the Cinque Ports; there is long-shore fishing, and periodically the Deal lifeboat makes heroic trips when ships are stranded on the Goodwins. Walmer Castle, south of Deal, is the official residence of the Lord Warden of the Cinque Ports (the gardens and the Duke of Wellington's room may be seen on certain days).
Dover 7 m. S.W.

DENHAM, Buckinghamshire.
Between the vast film studios and the busy Oxford road there still remains an unspoilt old-fashioned village complete with pond. Denham Place is 16th century, the Savoy 17th century, and the church 14th century.
Uxbridge 2 m. S.E.

DITCHLING BEACON, Sussex.
From its 813 feet is one of the grandest views over Weald and Down, and the 200-year-old windmill has long been a landmark. Ditchling Village has old houses, including one dated 1540 and given by Henry VIII to Anne of Cleves.
Brighton 8 m. S.

DORKING, Surrey.
Market town at the southern end of the gap worn through the North Downs by the River Mole, with Leith Hill (965 feet) to the south and Box Hill (590 feet) to the north-east. Disraeli wrote Coningsby at Deepdene, and George Meredith is buried in the cemetery. Keats finished Endymion at Burford Bridge (2 m. N.); and long before Juniper Hall became a centre for field studies, it sheltered General d'Arblay, who married Fanny Burney in the church at Mickleham in 1793. Dorking is one of the best centres for walking in this part of the country. Polesden Lacey (National Trust), 3 m. N.W., contains the Greville collection of pictures, tapestries, furniture, etc. House and gardens open to visitors on certain days. Reigate 5 m. E.

DOVER, Kent. 40.
In clear weather the French coast can be plainly seen from the heights – a sufficient explanation of the harbour and the castle. Nearby Blériot completed the first aeroplane crossing of the Channel in 1909, and Hitler's war demonstrated that cross-channel artillery bombardment and photography were also possible. Clearly a place of great consequence, and the Roman and medieval aspects of the castle mask a fortress of immense strength. Here, too, the cross-channel steamers come and go in the shortest sea route to the Continent of Europe.
Canterbury 15 m. N.W. Calais 21 m. S.

DUNGENESS, Kent. 56.
Low, sand and shingle point, jutting into the sea from Denge Marsh. An ornithologist's paradise. Lydd 4 m. N.W.

DUNMOW, Essex.
Dunmow's greatest gift to the world was the unsinkable lifeboat, perfected by Lionel Lukin in model form on what is known as Doctor's Pond. Little Dunmow is the scene of the annual 'trial' which, from 1244 to modern times of austerity, was the occasion for the award of a flitch of bacon to happily married couples.
Bishop's Stortford 9 m. W.

EASTBOURNE, Sussex.
One of the few 'planned' resorts on the English coast, the Duke of Devonshire having laid out wide streets and squares, with trees and gardens, between the old town and the lower slopes of Beachy Head. The Head is now claimed by the borough, which extends also to the east towards Pevensey, but gardens and music are still the keynote. In the old town, see St Mary's Church, the Lamb Inn and the Towner Art Gallery.
Hastings 14 m. N.E.

EGHAM, Surrey.
In contrast to its bustling neighbour, Staines, Egham is a quiet, dignified little place with a church containing memorials of the Barons who confronted King John with Magna Charta at neighbouring Runnymede, beside the Thames (National Trust). The Royal Holloway College (part of London University) contains a large and curious collection of English 19th-century paintings. Beaumont College is a Roman Catholic school for boys in a building that was for a time the home of Warren Hastings.
Staines 2 m. E.

EPPING FOREST, Essex.
Nearly 6,000 acres of beech, oak, birch and holly, now maintained as a public playground by the Corporation of London. Epping town still retains traces of the old days of horse coaches.
Waltham Abbey 4 m. S.W.

84

EPSOM, *Surrey*.
Famous for the racecourse over which the Derby and the Oaks are run, and for the mineral springs which provided a name for Epsom Salts. A busy little town with a wide market-place and a few buildings reminiscent of its 18th-century fame as a spa. Croydon 8 m. N.E.

ETON COLLEGE, *Buckinghamshire*. **39.**
Founded by Henry VI in 1440 with about 1,000 pupils, is one of the most important English public schools. Mellow red brick buildings with a magnificent 15th-century chapel of grey stone: acres of playing fields; riverside boathouses and the famous 4th of June procession; small top-hatted figures drifting along the busy High Street, as many world-famous men have done in their youth.
Windsor 1 m. S.

FARNHAM, *Surrey*.
A little market town near the western borders of the county. William Cobbett was born in the house now the *Jolly Farmer Inn*, and is buried in the church. Scott used the name of Waverley Abbey, now a beautiful ruin 2 miles east of the town, and Moor Park has associations with Swift, who here wrote *The Battle of the Books*, probably completed *The Tale of a Tub*, and met Stella. Farnham Castle, long the residence of the Bishops of Winchester, is now the official residence of the Bishop of Guildford. Farnham has many attractive Georgian buildings and some good 17th-century almshouses.
Guildford 9 m. E.

FAVERSHAM, *Kent*.
Pleasant old market town with shipbuilding and oyster beds on a creek connecting with the River Swale. The old Grammar School building is raised on arches, as is the Town Hall, and there are many picturesque timbered buildings. At Ospringe (1 m. S.W.), the old Maison Dieu is now a museum of Roman remains.
Canterbury 8 m. S.E.

FINGEST, *Buckinghamshire*.
Village among the hills at the head of the Hambleden Valley, with a notable church tower (Norman, with 13th-century saddle-back roof) peering above the trees. High Wycombe 6 m. E.

FOLKESTONE, *Kent*.
Enough remains of the old fishing town to indicate origins, but the modern seaside resort owes much to the fine cliff promenade known as the Leas. Wooded cliffs lead down to the sand-shingle beach, at the south-west end of which the sea-battered remains of Sandgate Castle can be seen above the waves. North-east of Folkestone the cliffs have slipped to form the Warren, a tangle of undergrowth worth visiting by botanists. Folkestone was birthplace of William Harvey, discoverer of the circulation of the blood. Dover 6 m. N.E.

Spraying fruit in Kent.

FOREST ROW, *Sussex*.
Small village on the infant River Medway amid fine scenery, including ruin of Brambletye, a Jacobean manor-house. At West Hoathly an interesting museum is in the 16th-century Priest's House. East Grinstead (3 m. N.) has many timber-built houses and a 17th-century Jacobean almshouse.
Tunbridge Wells 11 m. E.N.E.

GADSHILL, *Kent*.
Gadshill was Dickens's home from 1857 until his death in 1870. The house still stands, and is connected by a tunnel under the road with the chalet-summerhouse where he did much of his work. Rochester 2 m. S.E.

GLYNDEBOURNE, *Sussex*.
The mansion among the Downs is the home of Glyndebourne Opera Company, founded here by John Christie in 1934. Glyndebourne Music Festival is held in July each year.
Lewes 2½ m. W.

GOODWOOD, *Sussex*.
The beautifully situated home of the Duke of Richmond (open to visitors on certain days) has a collection of pictures by Van Dyck, Reynolds, Lely, Romney, Kneller, etc., and by the Smiths of Chichester. Goodwood racecourse is one of the loveliest in the country and in July is the scene of a very popular meeting. More recently motor-car races have also been held at Goodwood. Chichester 3 m. S.

GREENWICH, *London*. **37, 41.**
The Greenwich meridian – an imaginary line parting the eastern and western hemispheres and by means of which Greenwich time is calculated – originated in an order of Charles II. The Royal Observatory has recently moved to Herstmonceux (q.v.), but the old buildings remain.

The Norman pillars of St Bartholomew the Great, London.

Charles II also commissioned the Royal Naval College, though Wren made additions, including the Painted Hall. The National Maritime Museum occupies the Queen's house built by Inigo Jones. From points on Blackheath near the Observatory buildings are some of the finest views over London and down river beyond Woolwich.

GUILDFORD, *Surrey*. 28.
The town is firmly set in the gap worn through the North Downs by the River Wey. The High Street, on a hill with clock projecting from the 17th-century Guildhall, and other old buildings, is particularly attractive. St Mary's Church has Saxon work and medieval wall-paintings. Note Jacobean Abbot's Hospital. The keep of the Norman castle now forms a museum. Lewis Carroll is buried at Guildford. On the hill west of the town is arising the new cathedral designed by Edward Maufe, and beyond it stretches the ridge known as the Hog's Back.
Dorking 10 m. E.

HAMPSTEAD, *London*.
Bordering the Heath, and unsuspected by those who hurry along the main roads, are many lovely Regency villas with notable associations. In Keats Grove, in the garden of a house now forming a Keats Museum, the *Ode to a Nightingale* was written; artists from Romney and Constable to Henry Moore and Ben Nicholson have lived here, and the district is still an artistic and cultural centre. Constable is buried in the churchyard. The Heath has long been the most popular Cockney Bank Holiday resort. In addition to the Heath proper (highest point 440 feet), various adjacent open spaces increase the total area of open space to over 1,000 acres.

Kenwood House, designed by Robert Adam, surveys the Heath. It contains good collections of pictures and furniture, and is open to the public on certain days.

HAMPTON COURT, *Middlesex*.
The palace built by Wolsey on the Thames and given by him to Henry VIII is one of the finest of its kind in Europe. The west front is Tudor, but Wren made additions in the early 18th century. Pictures, armour, furniture, vast kitchens and wine cellars, a maze, and lovely gardens. Kingston 3 m. E.

HARROW ON THE HILL, *Middlesex*.
The spire of the 11th-century church is a Middlesex landmark. Clustering below the church are the buildings of the school, one of the two most important in England. The mellow red brick old school still remains, with the famous Fourth Form room, and with the library and the chapel, the War Memorial and the speech room form a notable group. Boarding houses are scattered along the ridge, and the Hill rises supremely above the suburban landscape.
Edgware 4 m. N.E.

HASLEMERE, *Surrey*.
Beautifully situated among wooded hills, close to Hindhead (850 feet), the Devil's Punchbowl and Gibbet Hill (National Trust). Here is a very good educational museum. The Musical Festival each July is noted for the medieval music played on old-type instruments under the direction and inspiration of the Dolmetsch family. Two miles south-east is Aldworth, built by Tennyson and where he died in 1892. Brookbank, at Shottermill (1 m. S.W.), was for a time the home of George Eliot.
Guildford 12 m. N.E.

HASTINGS & ST LEONARDS, *Sussex*. 17, 19.
Between the ruined Norman castle on the clifftop and the heavy architecture of James Burton still lingering in St Leonards, there is much verandahed Georgian building, and the subterranean promenade deserves to be seen. Not much is left of the old fishing town at foot of Castle Hill (pierced by St Clement's Caves). D. G. Rossetti was married in St Clement's Church. In Hastings, J. L. Baird made pioneering experiments in television. An all-the-year-round resort, sheltered by high ground.
Eastbourne 14 m. S.W.

HATFIELD HOUSE, *Hertfordshire*. 30.
Hatfield House, built in 1611 and the cradle of Elizabethan tradition, stands with its magnificent Tudor façades not twenty miles from London, easy access by coach and rail. Many of the great

figures of English history have been associated with it, and both Mary Tudor and, later, Elizabeth herself were kept prisoners in the royal palace of Henry VIII, of which one wing remains. This has now been transformed into a restaurant and tea-room for visitors who may see the famous pictures, gardens, and park, where the oak still stands beneath which Elizabeth was sitting when brought the news of her succession to the throne. Hatfield village has one or two old buildings from the days when it was a market town, but its chief feature is the church, with elaborate monuments to Robert Cecil, first Earl of Salisbury, and other members of the Cecil family.

HENLEY, *Oxfordshire*.
The annual regatta (June) provides a great concourse of amateur oarsmen. With its stone bridge and church tower, its wide market place and Georgian buildings, Henley is one of the pleasantest of riverside towns and the wooded Chilterns are background to lovely river views. Reading 6 m. S.W.

HERNE BAY, *Kent*. **42.**
The westernmost seaside resort in North Kent, with an unmistakable Victorian air that survives modern amenities and a pier three-quarters of a mile long. Reculver, on coast eastward, was the Roman *Regulbium* and later site of a 7th-century monastic church, the twin towers of which are preserved. Canterbury 7 m. S.W.

HERSTMONCEUX CASTLE, *Sussex*. 24.
Picturesque medieval brick mansion, restored in recent times and now the home of the Royal Observatory, so long at Greenwich. Hailsham 3½ m. S.W.

HIGH WYCOMBE, *Buckinghamshire*.
The older part is spread along the floor of the narrow valley of the River Wye, and has a lantern-crowned octagonal market hall and a very good Guildhall with cupola.
North of the town is Hughenden Manor, long the home of Benjamin Disraeli, and now in care of the National Trust (open daily). Bradenham Manor (2 m. N.W. across the hills) was the home of Isaac Disraeli, a lovely Elizabethan house described as 'Hurstley' in *Endymion*.
Wycombe is the centre of the Buckinghamshire furniture-making area, and specializes in chairs (chair-leg turning is a cottage industry for miles around); but with engineering, printing and other works it is fast becoming an important industrial town. Maidenhead 8 m. S.

HITCHIN, *Hertfordshire*.
A market town where peppermint and lavender are distilled. In the Old Meeting House (1691) is a chair presented by Bunyan. George Chapman, friend of Marlowe and Ben Jonson, was born here in 1559, and Eugene Aram was a local schoolmaster for a time. The church has a very good screen. Stevenage 4 m. S.E.

HODDESDON, *Hertfordshire*.
Here are a few remains of Rye House, celebrated in history as the birthplace of the plot to kidnap Charles II and the Duke of York. Haileybury College, a public school for boys, is now amalgamated with the Imperial Service College. Hertford 3½ m. N.W.

HORSHAM, *Sussex*.
A picturesque old market town round four cross-roads known as Carfax, where is still preserved the bull-ring. South from Carfax the Causeway, with many lovely old houses behind pollarded trees, leads to the church, with shingled spire. Two miles south-west is Christ's Hospital —the 'Bluecoat School' founded by Edward VI in 1552 and moved here from London in 1902. Field Place, 2 miles north of Horsham, was the birthplace of Shelley. Dorking 12 m. N.

HYTHE, *Kent*. 16.
Here the sea has receded, and the formerly active Cinque Port holds regattas on the canal built as a defence during the Napoleonic War. A modern seaside settlement lines the shingle beach. Westward high ground marks the ancient shoreline along to Lympne, where the Romans had a port of which Studfall Castle is the sole remnant. At Hythe is the principal School of Small Arms. In the church is buried Lionel Lukin (1742–1834), inventor of the self-righting lifeboat, and below the chancel is a remarkable bone crypt. From Hythe a miniature railway runs to Dymchurch and New Romney. Folkestone 5 m. E.

IGHTHAM, *Kent*.
A village much visited for the 14th-century manor house known as Ightham Mote (open on Fridays). Oldbury Hill, to the west, is a grand view-point. Here are remains of a prehistoric camp and some Stone Age rock shelters (National Trust). Sevenoaks 4 m. W. S.W.

JORDANS, *Buckinghamshire*. **31.**
The simple red-brick Quaker meeting-house (1688) had early associations with William Penn, who returned after founding Pennsylvania to be buried here, with members of his family and Thomas Elwood, Milton's friend. Jordans Hostel, a little above the meeting-house, incorporates a barn said to contain timbers from the *Mayflower*. Chalfont St Giles 2 m. N.E.

KEW, *Surrey*.
The botanical gardens adjoining Richmond Old Deer Park are the most beautiful and comprehensive in Britain. Here were raised, from Brazilian seeds, the plants which formed the nucleus of the Malay and Ceylon rubber plantations, and Kew introduced the quinine plant into India from Argentine. Kew Palace, within the gardens, is a pleasant house with relics of George III. Gainsborough is buried beside Kew Church. Just below Kew Bridge is Strand-on-the-Green, an unspoiled row of 18th-century houses. Richmond 2 m. S.

KINGSTON UPON THAMES, *Surrey.*
A modern shopping and residential centre with considerable boating activities, but which is also a very ancient place. See the Coronation Stone on which Saxon kings were consecrated, and the church, with 14th-century Lovekyn's Chapel. Across the river, Bushy Park with its famous chestnuts extends to Hampton Court Palace (q.v.). Richmond 4 m. N.

KNEBWORTH, *Hertfordshire.*
Bulwer Lytton (who lived and wrote here) considered that the partly rebuilt Tudor mansion had 'something of the character of Penshurst', and there is truth in the statement. Lytton and other memorials in the church.
Stevenage 3 m. N.

LAMBEF HURST, *Kent.*
A village of timbered houses which was once a centre of the Wealden iron industry. Two miles west are the ruins of 13th-century Bayham Abbey. One mile south are the ruins of 14th-century Scotney Castle.
Tunbridge Wells 6 m. N.W.

LEEDS, *Kent.* **26.**
The moated castle which received Froissart and was the prison of Richard II is still very impressive and the church has a tower that might well belong to a castle. By contrast the timbered houses of the village look toylike.
Maidstone 4 m. N.W.

LETCHWORTH, *Hertfordshire.*
The first 'garden city' in England. Well known for its printing and bookbinding, it also engages in engineering and other industries, but retains its residential atmosphere.
Hitchin 3 m. S.W.

LEWES, *Sussex.* **7, 13,** 27.
Venerable town with a ruined Norman castle guarding the defile by which the River Ouse passes between Mount Caburn (490 feet) and Mount Harry (639 feet), the latter the site of the racecourse and of the battle in which Henry III was beaten by Simon de Montfort (1264). In Barbican House, at the castle entry, is the museum of the Sussex Archaeological Society. Tom Paine lived in a house in the High Street; John Evelyn spent his boyhood at Southover Grange. Anne of Cleves's house at Southover is worth seeing, and opposite it Southover Church contains the leaden coffin of the Conqueror's daughter Gundrada. Brighton 8 m. S.W.

LULLINGSTONE, *Kent.* **14.**
The red brick Lullingstone Castle (open daily in the summer) stands in the unspoilt valley of the Darent. The owner now maintains a silk-farm here with mulberry trees. A small rich church alongside, with an interior of great beauty. Ancient timber in the park as well as an excavated Roman villa. Sevenoaks 6 m. S.

LYDD, *Kent.*
At the edge of the almost featureless shingly desert ending in Dungeness. The church, with its 130-feet tower, was bombed during the war, but there are good buildings of the days when Lydd was a port on the estuary of the River Rother. Lyddite, the explosive, was first made here. Rye 7 m. W.

MAIDENHEAD, *Berkshire.*
A shopping and residential town which is also one of the busiest centres of Thames boating. Just above the graceful 18th-century bridge is Boulter's Lock, and high among the woods on the opposite bank upstream is Cliveden, a famous house built in 1861 by Barry on the site of two others and including a fine 17th-century red brick terrace. The gardens are very lovely. Part of the house is still occupied by Viscount Astor, who presented it and the estate to the National Trust. (Visitors admitted on Thursdays in summer.) In the grounds is the Canadian Memorial Hospital. Windsor 5 m. S.E.

MAIDSTONE, *Kent.*
The capital of Kent stands either side of the River Medway – a busy road centre and market town with paper mills and breweries and some very good buildings. All Saints' Church is neighboured by the remains of the Archbishop's Palace, with an Elizabethan front and notable stables. Chillington manor-house (16th century) is now a museum. William Hazlitt was born at Maidstone in 1778, and pictures painted by him are in the art gallery. Cobtree Manor (2 m. N.) claims to be the original of Mr Wardle's House at Dingley Dell: it is now a popular Zoo park.
Chatham 8 m. N.

MALDON, *Essex.*
Old seaport at head of Blackwater or Maldon River estuary, still used by barges and small coasters, and a headquarters for sailing. The river waters are said to be the saltest round the British coast. Note 13th-century Moot Hall and three-sided tower of church.
Chelmsford 10 m. W.

MARGATE, *Kent.*
Though much visited by people from all over England, Margate is essentially the Londoner's resort – especially for day trips by boat. Here you may see Londoners-at play – either on the sands, or in the fun fair or around the harbour, or on the more select heights of Cliftonville. Sands, bands, cliff walks and a very bracing air. Canterbury 14 m. S.W.

MARLOW, *Buckinghamshire.*
Here the Thames tumbles over a long weir and is crossed by a suspension bridge. The charming old town has attracted many writers, from Shelley to J. K. Jerome (*Three Men in a Boat*). On the right bank of the river a little above Marlow Bridge is the Norman-towered church

of Bisham. The neighbouring Abbey (Tudor, restored) is now a recreation centre.
Maidenhead 4½ m. S.E.

MEREWORTH, Kent.
Mereworth Castle (1723-5) was built by Colin Campbell in imitation of Palladio's Villa Rotunda. The classical church (1744-6) has a steeple copied from St Martins-in-the-Fields.
Maidstone 7 m. E.

MICKLEHAM, Surrey.
A good village between chalk hills in the valley of the Mole. Admirable wooded scenery by the river. Dark mysterious yew woods by Cherkley Court and a famous group – the Druid's Grove – in Norbury Park. Note the aeroplane grave in the churchyard. See also under Dorking. Leatherhead 2 m. N.

MIDHURST, Sussex.
Picturesque market town adjoining the estate of Cowdray, in the park of which are some splendid old trees and the ruins of 15th-century Cowdray House, destroyed by fire in the 18th century. The present hall is 19th century. Polo is played here among lovely surroundings.
Chichester 10 m. S.

NEW ROMNEY, Kent.
On the edge of Romney Marsh (q.v.). An ancient Cinque Port now shrunk to a quiet town by the recession of the sea. Littlestone-on-Sea (1 m. E.) is a golfing resort with great coast protection works on either hand.
Rye 10 m. W.S.W.

OSTERLEY PARK, Middlesex.
An Adam mansion of brilliant red brick and rooms of the sharpest beauty. Formerly the home of the Earls of Jersey, but now National Trust. Just north of Osterley Station on the Piccadilly line.

PADDOCK WOOD, Kent.
The metropolis of the Kentish hop-fields, best seen in late summer, when hop-pickers and their families from London fill the great camp built for them and the massive array of oast-houses is so much more than picturesque structures.
Tonbridge 5 m. W.

PENSHURST, Kent.
A village beside the Rivers Eden and Medway. Penshurst Place may be seen on certain days and has a magnificent 14th-century hall and portraits of the Sidney family (Sir Philip Sidney was born here in 1554). Tonbridge 4 m. N.E.

PETWORTH, Sussex.
The narrow streets of the little town are dominated by Petworth House, the home of Lord Leconfield. The house is set in a magnificent park (open to public) and contains one of the finest private collections of pictures in England (notable landscapes by Turner). It was given to the National Trust by Lord Leconfield.
Arundel 10 m. S.

Gray's Monument, Stoke Poges.

PEVENSEY, Sussex. 51.
The Roman *Anderida* – one of the fortresses of the Saxon shore – is represented by a large walled enclosure. Here William the Conqueror landed in 1066, and there are considerable remains of a Norman castle. Eastbourne 4 m. S.W.

PILTDOWN, Sussex. 11, 12
A small village whose name is world-famous through the discovery in 1912 of the Piltdown skull. A monolith marks the spot.
Uckfield 2 m. S.E.

PULBOROUGH, Sussex.
A village on the Stane Street, among pastoral scenery which makes it an attractive headquarters for artists, and anglers.
Petworth 5 m. N.W.

RAMSGATE, Kent.
A blend of Regency crescents and modern fun fairs, a yacht basin, teeming sands, and a busy town: another of London's favourite seaside resorts. Offshore are the Goodwin Sands. Southward the low coast extends past Richborough to Deal. Margate 4 m. N.

RICHBOROUGH, Kent.
When Thanet was an island separated by a wide channel, the Romans built two of their forts of the Saxon Shore at either entrance, Reculver (*Regulbium*) at the north, Richborough (*Rutupiae*) at the south-east. The considerable remains of the Richborough Fort now look over fertile land where the channel has silted up; and there are now more than two miles of land between the fort and the sea. Sandwich 1½ m. S.

West Wycombe, Buckinghamshire.

RICHMOND, *Surrey.*
London's most popular Thames-side town and residential suburb. Many buildings take their tone from the remains of the palace built by Henry VII and in which Queen Elizabeth died. From the hill are very good views of the river, with Twickenham in the foreground, and beyond the *Star and Garter* is a magnificent park over 10 miles round. West of the park is Petersham, with Ham House (National Trust) a lovely example of 17th-century domestic architecture (Open to visitors on certain days.). See also Sudbrook House, Montrose House and Douglas House. George Vancouver, the explorer (1758–98), is buried in Petersham Church.
  Kew 2 m. N.

RICKMANSWORTH, *Hertfordshire.*
A prosperous dormitory town where the Rivers Gade and Chess join the Colne. The church has some good 16th-century glass. South of the town is Moor Park, with three golf courses and a mansion which once belonged to the Duke of Monmouth and was subsequently adorned with Corinthian portico and painted ceilings by Thornhill. Harrow 7 m. S.E.

ROCHESTER, *Kent.*
An ancient city with the ruins of a great Norman castle, with a tall square keep looking eastward across the River Medway to Chatham. The cathedral is on the site of a church founded by Augustine in 604; it is mainly Norman, and among the tombs and monuments is that of Bishop Walter, who founded Merton College, Oxford. Rochester was well known to Charles Dickens, and various streets, inns and buildings will be familiar to readers of his novels.
  Rochester is also the home of a great firm making flying boats. Maidstone 8 m. S.

ROMNEY MARSH. 16, 50.

ROYSTON, *Hertfordshire.*
Pleasant little town at the crossing of Ermine Street and the Icknield Way. The principal sight is a cave beneath the street in which are medieval carvings. Baldock 8 m. S.W.

RYE, *Sussex.* 16.
Rye is first seen from across the marshes – a cone of red-tiled roofs rising to the church tower. Within its ancient walls lie the packed cobbled streets of an unspoiled medieval town, once a mighty Cinque Port before the tide receded. Its ancient gateways, the Ypres Castle and *Mermaid Inn*, are but typical of the architecture found throughout the town. To find the sea you will need go to Rye Harbour, some two or three miles away, but the sea is still retreating. Henry James lived here. Hastings 9 m. S.W.

ST ALBANS, *Hertfordshire.*
The site of Roman *Verulamium* on Watling Street lies beside the River Ver south-west of the modern town. Vestiges of walls and tesselated pavements have been revealed, and an amphitheatre. There is a museum of Roman antiquities. On high ground is the cathedral, the church of the great abbey which grew around the sanctified remains of the martyred Alban. The great central tower is largely of Roman materials; there are impressive rectangular pillars in the nave and the transeptal clerestories have early columns. The shrine of St Alban behind the high altar was guarded by an oaken watching loft which still remains. West of the church is the gateway of the abbey. St Michael's Church, with Saxon work, is burial-place of the great Francis Bacon, Baron Verulam, who lived at Gorhambury – the ruins of his house adjoin the modern mansion. St Albans has a 15th-century clock tower, and the *Fighting Cocks Inn* is one of the oldest inhabited houses in England.
  Watford 6 m. S.W.

SANDWICH, *Kent.*
Sandwich is best entered by the chequered stone Barbican guarding the swing-bridge across the Stour. The town is medieval in appearance and in many of its customs: it was once headquarters of the Flemish emigrant weavers, and many of the buildings reflect their influence. One of the Cinque Ports, the sea is now two miles away, but its three churches, its Guildhall and many other good buildings bear witness to its bygone importance. Now famous as a golfing centre with its championship courses. Canterbury 11 m. W.

SEVENOAKS, *Kent.*
A very pleasant town with one of the oldest cricket grounds in England and a 15th-century grammar school at which George Grote was educated. Knole, one of the largest private houses in England, dates from 1456 and has

a wonderful collection of pictures and furniture. Given by Lord Sackville to the National Trust in 1946. See *National Trust List of Properties* for days on which it is open to visitors.
Tonbridge 6 m. S.E.

SHEPPEY, ISLE OF, *Kent.*
Between the Medway and the Swale rivers, with a naval port and garrison town at Sheerness, and at Minster (not to be confused with Minster in Thanet) an abbey church with a Saxon window and some good monuments.
Sittingbourne 3 m. S.W.

SHERE, *Surrey.*
Beautiful village among wooded hills: a first-class centre for walks and short excursions. A mile west the River Tillingbourne widens to form the lovely 'Silent Pool.'
Guildford 5 m. W.

SHOREHAM, *Kent.*
The most delightful village of the Darent Valley between swelling green hills. The house of the romantic painter Samuel Palmer (1805-81) is just below the bridge on the side of the Darent. His visionary landscapes of Shoreham scenery can be seen in the Victoria and Albert Museum and the Tate. Sevenoaks 5 m. S.

SHOREHAM-BY-SEA, *Sussex.*
Before the mouth of the River Adur became blocked with shingle (it now enters the sea about 1½ miles east), Shoreham was the principal port for the trade with Normandy, and it is in keeping that its church is one of the finest Norman buildings in Sussex. Earlier, trade had been conducted from Old Shoreham, a mile upstream: note church and old bridge.
    Well seen across the river is Lancing College (1848), a boys' public school. The chapel has some good woodwork, old and new, and pictures by Rubens. Brighton 6 m. E.

SITTINGBOURNE, *Kent.*
Market town amid cherry orchards, but making bricks and cement and paper. Milton, overlooking the creek connecting with the River Swale, has a church with a notable tower and some good old cottages. Chatham 8 m. N.W.

SOUTHEND-ON-SEA, *Essex.*
Thriving London dormitory and resort very popular with day trippers from London. The pier is nearly 1½ miles long. The borough includes Westcliff and Leigh – quieter and more residential. Brentwood 17 m. N.W.

STEVENAGE, *Hertfordshire.*
A long coaching town on the Great North Road with many Georgian houses, it is now one of the 'New Towns' being developed to relieve London's congestion. Hitchin 4 m. N.W.

STEYNING, *Sussex.*
Old-fashioned little town at foot of the Downs with a church having excellent Norman arches. At Bramber (1 m. S.) is a curious little museum. See p. 44. Shoreham 4 m. S.

STOKE POGES, *Buckinghamshire.* **89.**
Though so near to Slough and in an area rapidly becoming built up, the churchyard has still the air of peace which inspired Gray to write the *Elegy.* The adjacent field, with Wyatt's monument to the poet, is now in care of the National Trust. Slough 1½ m. S.

SUTTON VALENCE, *Kent.*
Picturesque village on a hill overlooking the Weald, with many Tudor cottages and a public school for boys. Maidstone 5 m. N.W.

SYON HOUSE, *Middlesex.*
Here, some ten miles out of Central London and across the river from Kew, is the notable mansion of the Duke of Northumberland, designed by Robert Adam. Good pictures and furniture. Open to the public on certain days. The grounds run to the river.

TENTERDEN, *Kent.* 16.
A delightful town of lovely buildings with an exceptionally wide-verged and tree-lined main street and a church with a fine shingled tower, from which tunes are played at each hour. Here was born William Caxton (1422), who in 1476 established at Westminster the first printing press in England. Ashford 10 m. N.E.

TONBRIDGE, *Kent.*
Pleasant market town with many timbered buildings including a 16th-century inn, a ruined Norman castle and a well known school for boys, founded by Cardinal Wolsey.
Tunbridge Wells 5 m. S.

TRING, *Hertfordshire.*
Straggly little town at the foot of the Chilterns, with a one-time Rothschild mansion possibly designed by Wren. The Zoological Museum is now a department of the British Museum of Natural History. Berkhamsted 5 m. S.E.

TUNBRIDGE WELLS, *Kent.*
Though it has long been better known as a residential centre than as a spa, the town retains many reminders of the fame its waters brought to it in the 17th and 18th centuries. The Pantiles is a unique raised promenade lined with shops. You can drink a cold cup of the waters at one end of the Pantiles. Good second-hand bookshops and antique shops are a feature of the town. Delightful rocky scenery round about. See also the superb ceiling in the 17th-century church of St Charles the Martyr.
Maidstone 14 m. N.E.

WALTHAM ABBEY, *Essex.*
Sadly hemmed about by indiscriminate modern buildings is the nave of a great abbey consecrated under Harold in 1060. The tower is a 17th-century addition, but the original work shows some of the finest Norman decoration in the country. A mile west, across the River Lea, is Waltham Cross, one of the monuments put up to mark the resting-place of Queen Eleanor's body as it was borne to Westminster Abbey. Both Abbey and Cross have given their names to modern industrial suburbs.
Edmonton 4 m. S.

WATFORD, *Herts.*
Market town. Important road and rail junction on the River Colne. Dormitory town on the Metropolitan Line. 'About Britain' Guides printed here. London 18 m. S.E.

WESTERHAM, *Kent.*
A village beside the infant Darent River. Quebec House (National Trust) was the birthplace of General Wolfe, and there is a statue by Derwent Wood on the green. 'Chartwell,' near Westerham, is the home of Mr Winston Churchill.
Sevenoaks 5 m. E.

WEST WYCOMBE, *Buckinghamshire.* **90.**
Bordering the narrow main road are so many good 17th- and 18th-century houses that to preserve them the Royal Society of Arts bought the whole village in 1929. It is now in care of the National Trust. The curious mausoleum and the striking classical church (1763) on the hill were built for the eccentric Lord le Despencer in 1763: the church was planned on the lines of a drawing room. Good views from the tower, and the adventurous may climb into the huge golden ball above it.
High Wycombe 2 m. S.E.

WILMINGTON, *Sussex.* **11, 27.**
Some mystery surrounds the origin of the huge figure of a man cut in the Downs. In the village are ruins of a 14th-century Priory, a very good tithe barn and a great yew tree in the churchyard. Eastbourne 5 m. S.E.

WINCHELSEA, *Sussex.* 17.
When the sea broke in upon Old Winchelsea (at the foot of the cliff) in the 14th century, Edward I set about building a fine new town with squares and streets – a plan rather in the grand manner; but some of the greatness of former days informs the church and the (later) houses of mellow red brick. Of the three gates,

the Strand Gate still spans the Rye road; the Land Gate guards the road to the railway station, and the New Gate stands ghostlike on the south.
Rye 2½ m. N.E.

WINDSOR, *Berkshire.*
Oldest existing royal residence in Britain, the castle dates from William the Conqueror, and the Round Tower still crowns the original Norman mound. Here Edward III in 1348 founded the Order of the Garter, and the Knights of the Garter still meet in St George's Hall and the lovely 15th-century St George's Chapel. Henry VI, Edward IV, Henry VIII, Charles I and all English sovereigns since George III are buried at Windsor, which also gives its name to the royal house. In the castle are very fine collections of Holbein portraits, and drawings by Leonardo, Michelangelo and Raphael.
The Town Hall near the castle gates is noted for the internal pillars inserted (against his will) by Wren. They do not, in fact, support the upper floor. The screen in the neighbouring church was adorned by Grinling Gibbons. South from Windsor the Home and Great Parks extend for 5 miles to the picturesque lake known as Virginia Water, with a cascade seen from the Exeter road. London 22 m. E.

WISLEY, *Surrey.*
Here are the extensive gardens of the Royal Horticultural Society, the premier gardening society of Great Britain – of the greatest interest for shrubs, flowers, vegetables, etc. Here new species and varieties are tried out. The public are admitted. Byfleet 1 m. N.

WITHAM, *Essex.*
Roadside market town with many pleasing houses and a church with a good rood screen. Centre of a rose-growing district.
Braintree 7 m. N.W.

WORTHING, *Sussex.*
While retaining its status as a holiday resort, Worthing has developed as a nucleus of a wide modern residential area with a genial climate and good Downland scenery within easy reach. It has associations with Richard Jefferies and W. H. Hudson (both of whom lie in Broadwater Cemetery, on the north of the town) and many more recent literary figures, and has a good repertory theatre. Sompting Church (2 m. N.E.) has a Saxon tower. Brighton 10 m. E.

WROTHAM, *Kent.*
Pleasant village at the foot of the North Downs. From Wrotham Hill above may be seen the great Weald in all its beauty.
Sevenoaks 6 m. S.W.